D1587811

TRADE AND INVESTMENT IN THE 1990S

JAPAN-U.S. CENTER
DISTINGUISHED LECTURE SERIES

VOL. I *Trade and Investment in the 1990s:*
Experts Debate on Japan-U.S. Issues
Edited by Ryuzo Sato, Rama Ramachandran,
and Myra Aronson

TRADE AND INVESTMENT IN THE 1990S

Experts Debate on Japan-U.S. Issues

EDITED BY Ryuzo Sato, Rama V. Ramachandran, AND Myra Aronson

Featuring Nobel Laureates Paul A. Samuelson, Merton Miller, AND James Tobin AND

Jagdish Bhagwati • Willem H. Buiter • Fujio Cho
Stephen Figlewski • Yasushi Hamao • Masahiro Kawai
Toru Kusukawa • Sadahei Kusumoto • Richard Levich
Joshua Livnat • Soshichi Miyachi • Thomas Pugel
Ryuzo Sato • Hiromoto Seki • Mike Synar
Hiroshi Tsukamoto • Masahiro Yoda
Richard Zeckhauser

THE CENTER FOR JAPAN-U.S. BUSINESS AND ECONOMIC STUDIES
Stern School of Business
New York University

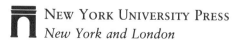

NEW YORK UNIVERSITY PRESS
New York and London

NEW YORK UNIVERSITY PRESS
New York and London

Library of Congress Cataloging-in-Publication Data
Trade and investment in the 1990s : experts debate on Japan-U.S.
issues / edited by Ryuzo Sato, Rama V. Ramachandran, and Myra Aronson.
p.   cm. — (Japan-U.S. Center distinguished lecture series ;
v. 1)
Includes index.
ISBN 0-8147-0641-X (acid-free paper)
1. United States—Foreign economic relations—Japan.   2. Japan—
Foreign economic relations—United States.   3. United States—
Commerce—Japan.   4. Japan—Commerce—United States.
5. Investments, Foreign—United States.   6. Investments, Foreign—
Japan. I. Sato, Ryuzo   . II. Ramachandran, Rama V.
III. Aronson, Myra   . IV. Series.
HF1456.5.J3T73   1996
337.52073—dc20   95.32525
                              CIP

CONTENTS

PART THREE Sanwa Lecture Series

PREFACE

As the first university-based institute to address the wide spectrum of issues facing Japan, the United States, and their trading partners, the Center for Japan-U.S. Business and Economic Studies has, from its inception, sponsored programs to promote dialogue between business leaders and academics on pertinent issues.

One of our forums has been a series of panel discussions moderated by Professor Robert Kavesh and featuring Nobel Laureate Paul A. Samuelson, Long-Term Credit Bank of Japan Visiting Professor of Political Economy. Joining in the discussion are business leaders from Japan and faculty members from the Stern School. In addition, every March the Sanwa Monograph Selection Committee meets to award a research grant for a monograph on international financial markets. The Committee consists of two Nobel laureates, Merton Miller and James Tobin, and Professors Akiyoshi Horiuchi, Ryuzo Sato, Marti Subrahmanyam, and Richard Zeckhauser. After the meeting the Committee participates in an open panel discussion in which they are joined by the General Manager of the Sanwa Bank, New York.

Our panels have become very popular, and are attended

regularly by students, faculty, and business leaders from the New York area. There have been repeated requests for transcripts both from those who attended the discussions and those who could not. In response, we are delighted to provide this book as the first volume in a series to be published by New York University Press. We hope you will find it both enlightening and entertaining.

RAMA V. RAMACHANDRAN, Associate Director
The Center for Japan-U.S. Business and
Economic Studies

PART ONE
Lectures from Fall 1993

CHAPTER 1

Bilateral Relations under New Administrations in Japan and the U.S.

September 23, 1993

INTRODUCTORY REMARKS

RYUZO SATO: As Director of the Center for Japan-U.S. Business and Economic Studies I would like to identify my Associate Director, Professor Ramachandran, and my Assistant Director, Myra Aronson, and also to take a few minutes to introduce our Center and our new Dean.

The Center is one of the first university-based organizations in the world to focus on understanding the entire spectrum of business and economic relationships between Japan and the United States. This is accomplished through research, teaching, publications, conferences, and other activities. I came to New York University from Brown eight years ago to become the first Director of the Center, and I am proud to say it is now recognized as the most active and the most successful of its kind. We have programs in all business disciplines, ranging from accounting, economics, finance, and information sciences to marketing and statistics.

For our NEC project on technology and competition we hold annual conferences in Tokyo and New York. Since 1986 Professor Paul A. Samuelson has held the Chair as Visiting Professor of Political Economy for the Long-Term Credit Bank of Japan's project on U.S.-Japan relations. The Sanwa Bank project relates to international financial markets, and we give a Sanwa Award every year for the best monograph in this field. Our TKC (TKC National Federation of Public Accountants) research project concerns economics, accounting, and data processing, and we also sponsor a comparative analysis of health economics in Japan and the United States. I heard President Clinton speaking about health reform last night. We are ahead of him by two or three years. We have held conferences and conducted several research projects on this subject.

We also edit an academic journal entitled *Japan and the World Economy* published by North Holland, for which we get submissions and subscriptions from all over the world. In addition to sponsoring research, we have tried to make the research results available to the public by holding conferences, panel discussions like the one we are having today, and also public lectures. We have many publications, most of which are published by Cambridge University Press.

Through the first eight years of the Center we had the support and guidance of Dr. Richard R. West, former Dean of the Stern School of Business. We are grateful for his leadership, and wish him a very productive sabbatical year. We are fortunate to have found someone as distinguished as Dr. George Daly to take over the helm as we begin our fall semester. A White House economist, his former deanship in Iowa was noted for the development of both fiscal and intellectual capital. He is also very committed to the kind of outreach for which we are present today.

GEORGE DALY: I'm delighted to welcome you to a conference devoted to the dissection of a problem. It is highly appropriate that it occur in this classroom, which so resembles an operating room.

I was commenting to our panelists before we came down here about a contribution that one of them, Professor Bhagwati, made to the *Wall Street Journal* recently. In it, he described a kind of divorce from reality that frequently occurs in dialogues of a political sort, particularly when they concern public policy, because no sensible politician, it seems, can afford to discuss any proposal that could possibly cause damage to anyone either directly or indirectly. I was struck by this phenomenon as I listened to President Clinton last night talking about the various good results that would come from his health care plan, reluctant to suggest that there were any people who might in fact be harmed by it.

The truth is that in the business world and in the real world we cannot afford such luxuries. The United States cannot, for example, continue to blame other countries for our own inadequate savings rate. This is not something that in the long term is going to serve us well either in a public or in a private sense. We need hardheaded and frank approaches to the difficult problems that confront us, and for that reason I am particularly pleased that our school can sponsor the kind of dialogue we hope to present today, one that will be both realistic and illuminating.

ROBERT KAVESH: We were reminiscing earlier about a panel appearance by Pat Choate, an outspoken writer and critic who appeared to have very little to say until he was literally forced to disgorge some material. I mention this in part because Professor Bhagwati was quoted in the latest *Business Week* as undermining some of Pat Choate's statements, criticizing a book that Pat Choate coauthored with Ross Perot. In any event, we are here today to continue the discussion on Japan-U.S. problems. Our theme is Bilateral Relations under New Administrations in Japan and the United States.

When a married couple gets into an argument and then the argument is settled, they raise glasses and toast to new beginnings. In a sense that's what we're talking about today. President Clinton has been in office the first 100 days, then the first 200 days (enamored by statistics, we count). In Japan we have the new administration of Mr. Hosokawa. I recently received a publication from the Metropolitan Museum of Art describing some panels the Museum had obtained. These panels had originally been in a building that the Hosokawa family built in the year 1606. So we have this ancient tradition in Japan, and in the United States we have Bill Clinton from Hope, Arkansas. It's an interesting cross section.

You look around. You see recessions in Japan, yes real recessions, reporting negative figures for growth in domestic product. In the United States it seems almost every day that we open our newspapers there is talk of 4,000 workers laid off, 9,000 workers laid off. In truth the number of people working continues to rise but still we're worried, and in Japan they're worried too. Arthur Schlesinger, two days ago in the *Wall Street Journal,* wrote about the futility of forecasting. The inevitable never happens. It is always the unexpected, as he quoted Lord Keynes. He didn't quote Paul Valéry, who said "the future isn't what it used to be." We worry, and sometimes we turn to angry words.

Just another moment of introduction. I returned two or three days ago from a trip to Scandinavia, a land of glaciers, snow, and many white, blonde people. I was with a group of Americans, most of them a bit older than myself (and I have been at this school for 36 years). Many of them were World War II veterans. During our trip we would frequently pass groups of Japanese tourists, and inevitably I would hear, "They are the ones who stole our jobs. They're the ones who stole our jobs." I was not there to fly the flag of the United States or of Japan, and I remonstrated with them a bit, saying, "You know, it's not quite that simple." But the language frequently deteriorated into name calling and the like, not in any outward way, but always this sort of grumbling, rah rah rah. This in the midst of the glaciers and fjords of Norway. So we have this problem: Bilateral relations under new administrations in Japan and the United States.

Our keynote speaker is Professor Bhagwati, an author who writes faster than most of us can read. He has had, and continues to have, a distinguished career. I can say nothing against him, except that I wish he were not involved at Columbia University.

As Prime Minister Hosokawa and President Clinton prepare to meet in New York on Monday, my thought goes back to another meeting, in Washington, between President Clinton and then Prime Minister Miyazawa. As I looked at the two of them standing together on the lawn of the White House, this diminutive Japanese Prime Minister and our gigantic and genial President Clinton, it occurred to me that obviously it was going to be very difficult for the two sides to see eye to eye. On the other hand, it was equally obvious that the situation could not possibly degenerate into an eyeball to eyeball confrontation.

I find it very hard to understand where the dialogue is at the moment. It reminds me of the joke where someone says that two people are not on speaking terms, to which the riposte is made: "That's not true. Just the other day I heard them shouting at each other!" It is important to understand the dialogue going on between the two sides, which is really quite tense, but I won't go into that because everybody is familiar with the facts. It has come to a stage in which I believe our administration needs to be rethinking the whole issue, and so should the Japanese.

I'm afraid that Japan policy is the only area of foreign trade in which the Clinton administration shows absolute clarity of purpose. I see more ambivalence with regard to other matters of trade policy. I was pleased, for example, when I heard President Clinton speak eloquently about suspending all our fears about NAFTA, touting the virtues of free trade and so on. Then he went on to say with equal eloquence that we had signed all these supplementary agreements on labor and environmental standards to raise the cost of production in Mexico. With one hand he was praising the virtues of free trade, and with the other he was buying into the same fears as Ross Perot (although not to the same degree). He was basically saying that the Mexicans should raise minimum wages and so forth, or else we could not have NAFTA. This attitude fundamentally flies in the face of free trade. You really don't want to have to say to other countries, poor countries, that they have to become our clones in terms of industrial costs. Surely he could have discussed other rationales for officially selling the supplemental agreements other than that otherwise we would have "unfair" trade. This acceptance and advocacy of the "unfair" trade rationale certainly undercuts the very basis of free trade.

So in my judgment there is some ambivalence in the President's thinking about trade issues such as NAFTA. But not on Japan. On Japan the administration has reached complete, unambiguous, nonambivalent clarity. I believe the policy is clearly wrong, and I will argue to that. Fear has become a dominant question in trade today. With poor countries, the fear is that by trading freely with them we will lose our wages or our jobs. With Japan, the fear is different. The general fear is that somehow we are not going to be able to compete successfully with Japan. Associated with this fear is the widespread view that the Japanese are wicked in some way. They are doing something we can't figure out. In short, they somehow "cheat" in trade to get ahead as well as they do.

The fear concerning Japan is different then. I think it arises partly from what I have called the Diminished Giant Syndrome, fueled by the economic rise of Japan and the Pacific nations. This fear is fundamental to our problems with Japan, and overlays the issues. Particularly in relation to market access problems, the Clinton administration has clearly moved toward wanting quick results, rather than saying, "Look, let's get to the fundamentals on this. Let's see if there are any regulations, etc., which are preventing market access. Could they shift perhaps to another set of policies where their social and other objectives are fulfilled but with less disruption of our market access?" Take retail distribution as an example. Could they subsidize the small-scale sector while allowing large-scale stores to open up, instead of simply stopping the free expansion of large stores in Japan? The development of large-scale stores would ease the way to market access for foreign businesses. At the same time, subsidize your mom-and-pop stores. Surely that is a better situation from our standpoint.

These are the kinds of things we should be discussing, rather than looking for specific commitments on how many stores will be opened up and when. But the administration has basically moved away from the discussion of institutional and policy measures aimed at improving our market access in Japan, which might open the way for the Japanese on their side to ask us how to ease their access problems in our markets. We go for "results." We ask for import targets, quantitative targets. Economists call this managed trade.

Managed trade just isn't the way we want to go in my opinion. I'm not speaking now as a theologian. U.S. Trade Representative Mickey Kantor, a shrewd negotiator, once made a celebrated remark saying he was interested in "results" and not in "theology." Now I don't think he meant by theology the taking of a degree from divinity school. I think he meant having a coherent analytical framework, which unfortunately we professors tend to inflict on ourselves when thinking about these issues. Once we come up with the proposition that we want to go for quantitative targets because we really don't know why Japan is not importing, we run into difficulties. We want to bypass all of that and just come out with "results" that would be close to what "true" market competition would yield. In reality, however, these results mean that some bureaucrat, some politician, some complainant in your own industry, comes up with some numbers and says, "This is the legitimate market share." This makes little sense. You wouldn't let your students decide what grades they should get, no matter how strongly they may feel about having been undergraded.

Economics is not that kind of precise science. Econometrics has not gotten to a state where you can really forecast with any kind of plausibility what a "true" market share would be. The one lesson in the postwar period is that any country that tries to plan that or think that way becomes impoverished. What is really needed is to set up an appropriate framework of policies and rules. In my opinion the administration, because of its panic on Japan, is moving exactly in the wrong direction. Import targets must mean that the Japanese government would get heavily involved. They could achieve these targets by cartelization and command—by first agreeing to targets, and then getting the industry to allocate those targets among different firms for fulfillment.

Similar to voluntary export restraints (VERs) there are what I have called voluntary import expansions (VIEs), that is, managed trade on the import side, just as VERs are managed trade on the export side. If you look at the history of the VERs they started out in specific sectors, judicially chosen and originally considered temporary. By now they have become a systemic problem worldwide, and we're trying to get rid of them. VIEs pose the same risk. They are also spreading. They started with semiconductors under the Republican administrations, and some people now want to extend them to autos and auto parts, and a variety of other sectors. Fred Bergsten wants them on twelve different sectors. The EU is saying that if we do this they will follow suit, because they expect that VIEs imposed at U.S. demand will lead to a diversion of trade from them to us because the Japanese will seek to accommodate us and politics will determine imports.

If you think, both in terms of historical experience and

in terms of the politics of the way these targets would be set, of the consequence for Japan, which is about to deregulate, of getting them to reregulate or to effectively use cartels in order to achieve these targets, you could lose sleep if you were a free trader and believed in rules-based trade. This is the way the French think. I have traveled with Arthur Duncal (former Director General of GATT). The French don't really study Professor Samuelson and then me, in that order, on international trade. They believe more in organized free trade, managed trade, and so on. Well, that's what has come to Washington now, because that's the way they think now about Japan.

So much for what we should not do. Let me now come to what we should do. We do have legitimate complaints, legitimate meaning politically articulate. Several industries say we can't sell in this market. We need a process by which we can handle these complaints, and it has to be a symmetric and impartial process. Article 23 of the GATT, for example, says you can bring up complaints. If you say, "Look, I can't sell pachinko parlors or computers in Japan," then you can go up before a judicial panel. I'm not saying they're going to be very well informed: there's very little jurisprudence on this. But jurisprudence will develop. Judges are never deterred from pronouncing on things for lack of existing jurisprudence. What you have there is an impartial process. If we say the Japanese aren't buying our auto parts because they've got a keiretsu supplier relationship, they likewise can take IBM to court saying "IBM is making its own chips; it is not buying from Hitachi." From a formal, economic point of view, a supplier relationship is the same thing as a vertically integrated process in economic theory models. The two are identical. It's only a legal difference.

What we really need is process. "It's the process, stupid," if I might borrow my phrasing from the Clinton campaign. Japan could be pushed around in my judgment because it needed to be pushed around in the early days when the country was closed. It was also economically and politically weak in those days. Today Japan is a superpower economically, and cannot be treated as if we can simply impose things on it by fiat and without regard to the impartiality and symmetry of trade dispute procedures. The process by which we deal with problems between us has to be symmetric, has to be impartial. Japan must indeed respond to our complaints, because they're real complaints and no administration can afford to ignore them. But we must go through fair and symmetric processes.

The surplus reduction target for Japan is equally problematic as a policy, and I'll conclude my remarks on that issue. I do think it is valid to argue that there is a deficiency of aggregate demand in the world today. There are also some underlying structural problems, but more than that right now, there is a deficiency of aggregate demand.

In the United States, as doubtless you know, the 1980s left us with a high debt-GNP ratio. We've got a current-account budget deficit as well. Our capacity to use fiscal policy to do anything to add to the world demand is simply handicapped. President Clinton's first budget illustrated this problem well. The EU has the same problem. The Japanese are in a position to be able to spend more, because they don't have these two handicaps. They followed fiscal prudence during the 1980s.

We should therefore urge the Japanese to increase fiscal spending. This is not to condemn their surplus, because the surplus is not in itself a bad thing. A surplus can in fact mean supplying savings to the rest of the world, where there is so much shortage of savings everywhere now — to India, the old USSR, the Middle East, for example. Because of our spending propensities, however, we are not in a position to supply savings to anyone. Why should we then condemn the Japanese surplus, which is in fact a wonderful gift to the savings-hungry world? But we don't want to say, "Look, you have the capacity in the short run to reflate the world economy, to become the locomotive, so please exercise some leadership and spend more." We don't want to think and talk in terms of the surplus, because the external surplus is simply neither here nor there in itself. As soon as we focus on that, we give currency to Gephardt and others who mistakenly argue that the surplus means Japan is closed. That, of course, is a fallacy. There are marvelous quotes on these matters from the Congress and now from the Clinton administration for our students to analyze, not condemn.

Such thinking is wrong. The targeting of the surplus is wrong for reasons of principle. You can target fiscal policy, monetary policy, but not the consequences, because you could expand and still not have the same impact on the surplus. Moreover you don't know what the exact effect will be, even if you think it will reduce the surplus. If Prime Minister Hosokawa agrees to targets on external surplus reduction and it doesn't happen, even if he's done all the things like expansive fiscal policy, Gephardt will be at him again. Hosokawa would be a fool to sign up for such a target in my opinion, since it would create more problems down the road. Everything we are doing on the Japan trade issue is wrong, fundamentally wrong. The Japanese have to exercise leadership by acting as the world's locomotive. Even if they do, it's not going to have a big effect, but at least it can help.

My agenda for the time being then would be for the Japanese to continue resolutely saying no to targets on both trade and on surplus reduction. I think they have been saying no, but I suspect that the Japanese no is frequently understood as a Japanese yes. I hope it's a clear and resounding no this time. At the same time there should be a yes, a clear resounding yes, on shifting action to the GATT, on making a lot of concessions in a reciprocal framework at the GATT. There should be a yes to taking a substantially augmented fiscal and monetary expansion to help both the world economy and themselves, for they would be beneficiaries as well. I think that's where we want to put the new agenda. If we do that, we are strengthening multilateralism. We would in fact reflate the world economy, and multilaterally strengthen all the good values. It would mean having a symmetrical relationship between the two parties. You can't push Japan around in my judgment. It's ridiculous. Because it's so obvious, however, I'm not sure it will be done.

ROBERT KAVESH: Our next speaker is Hiroshi Tsukamoto, the first of our two Japanese representatives. Currently President of the JETRO Company in New York, he comes to us with 24 years' affiliation with Japan's Ministry of International Trade and Industry (MITI).

Professor Bhagwati said that Prime Minister Miyazawa and President Clinton had a difficult time making eye-to-eye contact. But when our Prime Minister Hosokawa meets with President Clinton in New York in the fall of 1993 I think both of them will find it easier to have eye-to-eye contact, because Mr. Hosokawa is a bit taller than average. I also think he will come here representing new perspectives for Japan, and I believe the two leaders can deepen their mutual understanding on this occasion.

Many people in the U.S. today like to hear the word "change." Like Dean Daly, I was also very interested in President Clinton's message yesterday on the reformation of health care. Such reform is clearly a difficult thing to accomplish. A politician always has to use a soft word to cover reality, and the true reality is never easy. I see many good signs pointing to change in the U.S. today, and I also would like to elaborate on some of the changes in Japan.

First I would like to quote Sakaiya Taichi, who is a very famous columnist as well as a former MITI official. He is a very sharp analyst of the current prospects for Japan's economy. Taichi argues that change in Japan is realized very slowly. Nevertheless, company people—business people—can change more quickly than most. Based upon experience, business people seem to take five years to implement changes. Politicians take ten years to bring about change, and bureaucrats take fifteen. Since I come from MITI myself, I really should understand the meaning of his message: Any organization, if it is well established, is very difficult to change. But I think that Japan is now coming to a turning point.

Professor Samuelson took part in a symposium several years ago in Japan in which the concluding remarks to his Japanese audience concerned his expectations for Japan in the nineties. He said he expected some kind of coexistence between ruthless efficiency and humanity, although this would be a difficult thing to promote. We Japanese understand the importance of his message.

In MITI, although it is very difficult to predict the future, every decade we launch an "Industrial Vision." In the seventies and eighties we were promoting knowledge intensification, but our key words for a vision of the nineties have to do with creating human value in the global age. Why do we urge the importance of creating human value? Once we thought concentration on accumulating wealth was enough, and during the catch-up period of our economy we took the accumulation of wealth very seriously indeed. But now that Japan is relatively rich, the important priority has become her role in the global environment. More efforts must be made to work toward global welfare and security. At the same time, we seek a more balanced way of life for the Japanese people. This is the message from MITI concerning our vision for the nineties.

This is not an easy target to pursue. The older generation still perceives our people as the inhabitants of a very tiny island with very limited resources. Under these circumstances, hard work is the only way to promote Japan. But I belong to a younger generation, not so far from President Clinton's. Before I came here I was the Director of the Policy Planning Office at MITI. I was responsible for long-term industrial policy strategy. My generation is thinking in new ways, and we believe that the single-minded accumulation of wealth is not a good thing. We believe in the importance of economic balance.

This is not to exempt ourselves from the severe criticism we have sustained from foreign countries. It is in our own best interest to move in this direction. The future of any country lies in the creativity of its people, and in order to enhance that kind of creativity it is better for the economy to function in a more balanced way. Although this kind of strategic change is very difficult to accomplish, our new Japanese leaders are trying to promote it on a meaningful level—we are talking about something more substantial than the concept of a "kinder and gentler nation."

I don't have enough time to elaborate on all the kinds of changes that are occurring in Japan. I do believe that the Hosokawa administration's new thinking, combined with our amply seasoned economic tradition, will force us to change the structures by which we operate. Japanese industry will increase overseas production, for instance, because of the appreciation of the yen. Price competition in the Japanese market will become ever more fierce in the face of our depressed economy. Many consumers are already placing more emphasis than before on the price of goods. Deregulation will accelerate market competition as well. Deep innovations will be sought to accomplish these changes. Even with all of this, Sakaiya Taichi reminds us that change is a real struggle, and it will take time. But please understand that we are going to change.

ROBERT KAVESH: In the Prologue to Heaven in Goethe's *Faust,* it is written that "a good man through obscure aspirations has still a notion of the one true way." In a sense we are here today looking for, if not the one true way, then several true ways. It is my pleasure to introduce Ryuzo Sato, who is not only the Director of our Center but Professor of Economics here at the Stern School and a wonderful colleague.

1993 was a year of great political change in both Japan and the United States. Bill Clinton replaced George Bush in the White House, and Morihiro Hosokawa became Prime Minister of Japan. Much has been made of the fact that this is the first Democratic administration in twelve years, Clinton is the youngest President since John Kennedy, and Hosokawa is the first non-LDP (Liberal Democratic Party) Prime Minister in 38 years. But more important than these superficial changes is the change in values they represent. An understanding of these values is likely to be crucial to understanding the personality of the Clinton administration, and may also offer insights that will help us predict the future direction of U.S.-Japanese relations.

Several years ago when reporters asked Crown Prince Naruhito to describe the qualities he was looking for in a future wife, he replied, "I want to marry someone who has the same sense of values that I have." Although the concept of values is taken very seriously in both the United States and Europe, it has attracted little public attention in Japan until recently. Even the expression that means "values" in Japanese is not very old. If we think about it, however, frictions are bound to arise in any relationship— be it a marriage or a relationship between two countries— if the two partners have major differences in priorities, in the things that each side considers important in their lives. If partners don't share similar values, they will have to spend enormous amounts of energy reaching an agreement.

Bill Clinton is the first President of the United States to be born after World War II, and his administration reflects the values of the baby-boom generation. How can this be expected to affect U.S.-Japanese relations? First, this administration will not be bound by ideology or labels, but will be results-oriented. This will mean a tougher policy toward process-oriented Japan. Japan will be told to show results, not to try to get by with explanations or excuses.

Furthermore, the participation of women in public affairs will be greater than ever. Barbara Bush was famous for being a good wife in the traditional sense of the word, devoted to playing a supportive but clearly subordinate role to her husband. Hillary Rodham Clinton projects the image of the modern career woman with abilities and values of her own, capable of carving out a position for herself independent of her husband's status or occupation. In the same sense, the fact that career woman Masako Owada will one day become Empress might provide the rest of the world with some new insight into Japan. The Japanese sense of values may not be quite so different as some people have tended to believe.

Although I have used the expression "a change in values" to describe the new administration, that does not mean that everything has changed overnight. Life, liberty, and the pursuit of happiness, the fundamental concepts on which the United States was founded, remain a constant source of American values despite the transfer of power. Still, the weight given to each of these human rights in a given administration reflects the political philosophy, conservative or liberal, of the President in power. If the Bush administration could be defined in terms of Hamiltonian elitism, President Clinton's political shading might be called Jeffersonian populism. This liberal spirit reveals itself in policies that show greater tolerance toward people of color, women, the socially disadvantaged, and homosexuals.

Another aspect of U.S. policy that is central to our current discussion of U.S.-Japanese relations is the view that began to emerge in the late 1980s of economic strength as a national security issue. The fact that President Clinton has set up a new cabinet-level National Economic Council on the model of the already existing National Security Council is a clear sign that he intends to treat economic policy on the same footing as military strategy. Because Clinton believes that America's future depends on a revitalization of the U.S. economy, his administration will approach the issue of strengthening and raising America's international competitiveness as the economic equivalent of war.

Three months have passed since power changed hands in Japan for the first time in thirty-eight years, and a new ruling coalition formed a new government headed by Prime Minister Morihiro Hosokawa. Whenever I say that

I first came to the United States as a graduate student in 1957, the response I get from most people is: "That's a long time ago." But the Liberal Democratic Party's one-party rule in Japan began even longer ago than that, in 1955. During that long period of time, one government succeeded another as each faction of the party took its turn in the seat of power. But for the Japanese people, the expression "a change in government" only meant that another group of old men in morning suits would meet the Emperor and have their pictures taken. They were resigned to the fact that nothing else would change.

The present change of government has therefore created a great deal of excitement. A first-time Diet member has become the Prime Minister; a woman has been appointed Speaker of the House for the first time in Japan's history; and the cabinet, with the sole exception of the Minister of Foreign Affairs, consists entirely of newcomers who have never held cabinet posts before. What is perhaps most significant about the present change is that it has aroused the interest of the Japanese people in their government and raised their expectations. It has also made some Japanese politicians and bureaucrats very nervous.

Members of the Liberal Democratic Party, who now find themselves in the opposition, talk about the fragility of the new ruling coalition; but popular support for the new government exceeds 70 percent, the highest in post-war history. By comparison, Prime Minister Takeshita had a popularity rating of 5 percent and Miyazawa's was 9 percent at the end of their terms of office. The 70 percent approval rate is a clear indication of how high popular hopes are for change.

Among the tasks facing the new government, the most important are political reform and policies to stimulate Japan's flagging economy and reduce its ever-expanding trade surplus. For this audience the issue of political reform in Japan, I suspect, is a purely domestic problem. With this in mind, I will focus my remarks on Japan's economic stimulus policies, particularly deregulation and the trade surplus problem, both of which have a profound impact on the relationship between the United States and Japan.

U.S.-Japan relations can be thought of as having entered a new stage this past summer, when the exchange rate approached the 100 yen to the dollar level. Although there is much talk about the 100 yen barrier, sooner or later it, too, will be broken if the trade surplus continues to rise. This means that Japanese businessmen, just like Japanese politicians, are being forced to make fundamental changes whether they like it or not.

Metaphorically speaking, the strong yen and Japan's trade surplus are related to one another in much the same way as cholesterol is to high blood pressure. An abnormal buildup of the trade surplus causes the yen exchange rate to rise. In the economy, just as in the human body, any imbalance immediately sets off a warning signal. What has pushed the value of the yen up to its present heights is the obstinate assertion within Japan that the trade surplus is good for Japan and the world economy as well. This argument, advocated mostly by economists in the Japanese ministries, has temporarily been silenced as the trade surplus has brought Japan's economy to a state of near paralysis. But the policy errors committed in its name have been serious ones.

Until recently Japanese government spokesmen, especially those in the Ministry of Finance and the Ministry of International Trade and Industry, used to claim that an enormous trade surplus was a healthy phenomenon. Having a trade surplus was natural for an economic superpower, they believed, citing countries that had dominated the world economy in the past such as the British Empire before World War II or the United States during its golden age after the war. The pitfall in this argument is that it ignores the fact that the American market in its heyday was open and very competitive.

In a market free of any artificial manipulation, a trade surplus may in fact be a sign of comparative advantage. Moreover, because the U.S.-led economic system after World War II operated under a fixed exchange rate until the middle of the 1970s, currency values were not driven up to extreme levels in countries with a trade surplus. It is ridiculous to apply these special circumstances to present-day Japan as justification for running up a trade surplus. It has also been argued that because Japan's trade surplus is invested in other countries and enriches the global economy in this form, it should be thought of as Japan's contribution as an economic superpower to international society. Given the present upward trend of the yen, however, no Japanese investor would seriously consider buying foreign bonds and securities. In any event there is no point in trying to track down the culprit responsible for the current recession, which has resulted from the strong yen. What both the Japanese government and the Japanese business world should be searching for instead are ways to work out effective measures that can deal with these new realities.

The present recession has led to a decline in imports, which in turn has led to an increase in the trade surplus. This chain of events is not merely the result of a business cycle. It has been caused by the unhealthy state of the Japanese economy. The Hosokawa government diagnosed the situation correctly when it recognized this fact and included deregulation as part of its economic stimulus plans. The strong yen, of course, applies the brakes to Japan's export initiative. The question is whether internal demand can be expanded enough to make up the difference. There has been much talk recently about generating internal demand from the private sector, but in order to do so resolute efforts must first be made to ease regulations and pass the benefits of the strong yen on to the consumer. Let me give you a few concrete examples.

1. Although Japan's expensive rice has come under attack worldwide, the high cost of cosmetics is a surprisingly well-kept secret. The reason Japanese toiletries are so costly, it is commonly acknowledged, is that retail prices set by makers of consumer goods are particularly binding in the cosmetics area. On July 28 the national newspapers

reported that Kawachiya, a discount chain, filed a complaint with the Monopoly Commission charging that it had been unfairly suspended from doing business as an outlet affiliated with Shiseido and Kanebo, Japan's two leading makers of brand-name cosmetics, and had been subject to restrictions on delivery in violation of the Antitrust Act.

2. Any Japanese who travels to the United States or to Europe is aware of the astonishing variety of locally brewed beers. Germany is said to have as many brands of beer as there are valleys to brew them in. The same is true in America. The family of a colleague at my university runs a restaurant in the western United States. The restaurant enjoys a good reputation, and he proudly told me that his family had recently begun to brew beer in its cellar. In Japan, however, such private brewing of beer is not permitted. Robert Samuelson touched on some of Japan's nontariff barriers in a column in the June 21, 1993 edition of *Newsweek*. As a concrete example, Samuelson cites beer imported at a cost, say, of ¥100. Though the official tariff is only ¥2, somehow the price is increased by the invisible tariff of ¥143 so that the beer costs ¥243 when it finally appears on the market. What has particularly stirred up the U.S. side is that this study was done by two Japanese economists, Professors Yoko Sazanami and Shujiro Urata, for the Washington-based Institute for International Economics.

3. The Japanese system of car inspections (Shaken-system) has frequently been pointed to as pretty strange.

Once a car is three years old it must undergo inspection every two years. After ten years annual inspections are required. The cost of these inspections (ranging from $800 to $1,500) is much higher than the cost of a safety check in the United States. Even though Japan prides itself on making the best and safest cars in the world, it demands that all car owners in Japan submit to these periodic inspections. Clearly there is a contradiction at work here.

Although there are no tariffs on foreign cars, they are far more expensive in Japan than in Europe. I was told this is because of the high prices set by the manufacturers, who take advantage of the fact that high-priced goods sell well in Japan. The poor Japanese consumer is treated with contempt even by foreign manufacturers. In short, the Japanese consumer is made a fool of by foreign manufacturers and Japanese officials alike, and ends up living with the highest prices in the world.

4. Although not a government regulation, authorization must be obtained for a cab driver to pick up passengers in front of a railroad station; otherwise the cab driver cannot do so—even when there is a long line of people waiting for taxis. The grounds on which this authorization is granted are far from clear. The decision is made behind closed doors, and the right to pick up passengers at railway stations is conferred on taxi drivers in much the same way as the right to bid on public works projects is conferred on contractors. The people who are inconvenienced by this system are the poor commuters, who see the empty cabs right before their eyes yet are not allowed

to get into them. Even a partial attempt to ease these strange regulations and cozy agreements that protect producers and suppliers at the expense of consumers will make the lives of the Japanese people far more comfortable.

Examples of unnecessary regulations such as those I have just cited abound. Creating from within an entrepreneurial spirit that energetically promotes free competition and an open market and brings about an improvement in the way Japan does business will lead to economic recovery and to a reduction in Japan's trade surplus. The recession in Japan right now is very serious, and prospects for the immediate future seem quite murky. At last the Bank of Japan announced a cut in the official discount rate to 1.75 percent, the lowest in Japan's history (compared to 3 percent in the U.S. and 6 percent in Germany). Deregulation and macroeconomic policy are the two indispensable elements in any attempt to expand the economy and thereby reduce the trade surplus.

ROBERT KAVESH: George Stigler, who won the Nobel Prize in Economic Science (somehow economic science does not flow trippingly from the tongue), wrote an article years ago called "Competition Yes, But." In it he catalogued all the claims and demands that people have for special treatment, which is of course part of our discussion today. In introducing Paul A. Samuelson I am really sharing my own history, my own youth, my own maturing. Paul, was

"The Interaction of the Acceleration Principle and the Multiplier" your first published piece? It wasn't. But I remember reading that and wrestling with what I thought was its arcane mathematics. Little did I know what was in store over the years in terms of economic science. In any event I give you Professor Samuelson, the Economist of the Twentieth Century, and as far as I'm concerned the Nineteenth, Eighteenth, and Seventeenth Centuries as well. The Great Man. The Nobel Laureate, and first American ever to receive it in Economics.

PAUL A. SAMUELSON

I have a literal mind. When I see the title for today's discussion, namely "Bilateral Relations under New Administrations in Japan and the U.S.," the word "bilateral" reminds me of the economic theory of the balance of payments. Economists, you see, are just like Pavlov's dogs: Ring a bell and the conditioned dog salivates. Say the right word and the conditioned economist begins to babble about elasticities of supply and demand.

Presidents and Prime Ministers are not like that. They go whole hours not thinking about economics. Fortunately, Jagdish Bhagwati wears bifocal glasses, so to speak. He can take the telescopic view of politics and history; and yet, when the problem presents itself, he can juggle J-shaped curves and Marshall-Lerner conditions with the best of us. Ryuzo Sato, when he is not winning Japanese Pulitzer prizes for perceptive books on our two societies, slugs away at the mathematical economics of conservation laws and technological change. Having Hiroshi Tsukamoto here is indeed a bonus: It is like getting an account of biblical Genesis from one of the angels who was in on the Creation.

Now down to business. In 1992, when the German and Japanese locomotives were idling in the station, the American macroeconomic locomotive was propelling U.S. GDP forward at a 3.8 percent annual rate while, at the same time, helping support the world economy. As Will Rogers said, "No good deed goes unpunished." Were we rewarded to have Europe and Asia join us in 1993 by also engineering expansionary progress? Not at all. The bilateral deficit between America and Japan has reached new peaks. Whatever the intentions of President William Clinton and the new Prime Minister Morihiro Hosokawa, de facto the weak Japan GDP is eroding U.S. exports to Japan at the same time that our degree of recovery is pushing upward what we import from Japan. Good intentions and lofty sentiments cannot head off increasing frictions ahead.

No wonder the dollar depreciates. Lynching a few speculators will not solve the problem. Army surgeons know that God and Darwin rely on maggots to clean out the wounds of battle. Not very edifying, but that's the way things are. Speculators are the maggots that God and Darwin rely on to clean up disequilibria. An Invisible Hand, so to speak, leads them to accomplish what is no part of their intention. Let's not go overboard praising those worms. Thanks to the vanity of governments, and their plentiful endowment of stupidity—I mean especially French governments!—the speculators on balance get well rewarded for their efforts. (I like to quote that sage of Omaha, Warren Buffet, the richest man in the world, who started out with an MBA from the Columbia Business School. In one of his memorable Berkshire-Hathaway annual reports, Buffet observed: "If you are in a strange poker game and within half an hour you haven't located who is the patsy—you are." Governments are like the Bourbons: They learn nothing, and they forget nothing. They go decades not recognizing who the patsies are in the game of international finance.)

For almost 40 years now, the harmony of Japan-U.S. political relations has been strained by the irritant of a continuing and growing bilateral payments deficit. Of course, economists never consider bilateral balance as the desideratum of policy. If Japan were in deficit with third parties who were in equivalent deficit with us, that would be an even more efficient geographical division of labor.

Overall current balance is itself no proper goal of policy. When America before 1914 was growing the way Korea was growing in the 1970s, it was optimal and not aberrant for the developing society to be importing productive capital goods and paying for them by IOUs or other forms of capital contracts. Some chronic patterns of multilateral current imbalance are signs of healthy equilibrium and not of pathology or predation.

Indeed, we know from the Ohlin-Keynes literature on the transfer problem that a sizeable Japanese surplus could be recycled by prudent investing in American assets, to the benefit of both regions; and that this could conceivably transpire under unchanged commodity terms of trade and without any dollar depreciation relative to the yen. Yes, many things promised by the Tooth Fairy can turn out to be true: Dollars under pillows and giant molars sure to come.

Japan has come to adulthood. I often say that the advantages of being grown up should not be exaggerated; that there are only two as far as I can observe. As an adult you can always play with new tennis balls; and you don't have to finish what's on your plate. There's not much else. Seriously though, for Japan to be an adult is to have the power of consent, which means also the power of dissent and refusal. There was nothing wrong with the title of the book, *The Japan That Can Say No* (Shintaro Ishihara and Akio Morita, Simon and Schuster, 1991). What was defective were the issues and arguments in the book's pages about what Japan should turn tough on. One of the privileges of being an adult is that you have the right to act childlike. But does an adult, on reflection, really want to be self-destructive?

Some Japanese opinion leaders say, at least among themselves: "If Americans privately save much less than the Japanese, and under Reaganomics publicly dissave enormously, then economic law and basic arithmetic dictate that the high-consumption region must have a net capital deficit and the higher-saving region must have a net capital surplus. So, what is all the bellyaching about?"

True enough, and I was one of the first to stress how macro law must work out. Belligerent Americans, at least in private, similarly sometimes say: "So long as Japanese investors will spontaneously want to recycle that surplus by buying up American skyscrapers, golf courses, and even Brooklyn Bridges—then there need be no uncomfortable appreciation of the yen to challenge and vex Japanese producers. So, what is all the bellyaching about when the dollar floats down from 260 to 104 yen to the dollar because Japanese investors behave otherwise?"

One country cannot dictate to another what its folkways and mores must be. If Japanese want to save, who is to say them nay? If Japanese truly prefer their own kinds of production, who has the right to tell them how to spend their legally earned incomes? If everywhere technology were appropriate for deregulated laissez-faire, then changing Schumpeterian knowledge and dynamic preference alterations could still certainly harm and benefit different regions differently both in quality and quantity. If all governments had long since subscribed in full measure to GATT's purest of free trade, one could imagine an international order in which no sovereignty was accorded the right to complain or ask for interferences to redress the fortuitous loss of previous advantage.

We do not live in such a world. No one comes into the Court of World Opinion with clean hands on issues of free trade. De facto and de jure, we live in an interdependent community of mixed economies. American resources are depended on to help protect the security of Europe and Asia. So long as a potential activistic macroeconomic program by the Bank of Japan and the Ministry of Finance can have helpful effects on Japan and at the same time have significant external effects on America, it is rather natural that our leaders and citizenry should pontificate against passive and belated actions by these Japanese agencies. While the Japanese political system manifestly has the right to shrug off such external preachings and criticism, the question we must each ask of our adult selves is this: Do we want to stand on our rights to do whatever we wish, when experience and reason suggest that doing so is likely in the end to be self-destructive at home and needlessly harmful abroad? The grown-up Japan that can say no, I am arguing, should be the canny and friendly Japan that can often say yes, and not infrequently say maybe.

Germany and Japan are often bracketed together in criticism at not pulling their macroeconomic weight. I have no sentimental sympathy for the Bundesbank, but I think such bracketing is unfair to Germany. After reunification of East and West, Germany does have some special problems that stagnating France and Japan do not have. M3 does grow fast in Germany. Supply shocks from the Eastern zone do involve inflation fears that are not necessarily paranoid. So Germany's slowness to reduce interest rates and save the European Currency Union is understandable, even if perhaps not forgivable.

But Japan's folly is self-inflicted. The new head of the Bank of Japan, apparently, does not know his trade. The bureaucrats from Tokyo University Law School never did know economics, and they have autonomously adhered to fiscal austerity after it ceased to be desirable. The old LDP knew precious little about economics. Alas, the new Coalition has so far shown little better sense, either in deed or in utterance. I hope NYU economists can do a good turn for Japan in the future by persuading a change in opinion, just as MIT economists did France a favor when our letter to the *Financial Times* helped destroy the pegged EC parties that were asphyxiating France, Britain, Italy, and Spain.

CHAPTER 2

Trade Negotiations and Agreements: A Trend toward Further Liberalization

October 18, 1993

INTRODUCTORY REMARKS

ROBERT KAVESH: There are few topics of more importance in today's economic world than international trade, trade negotiations, and trade agreements. It's a wonderful time to teach microeconomics, because the front page of the newspaper is filled with all kinds of trade issues—and other pages of the newspaper are as well.

We are fortunate today to have a very distinguished panel with us to discuss Trade Negotiations and Agreements: The Trend toward Further Liberalization. Congressman Mike Synar will give a view from Washington of NAFTA and its implications for the rest of the world; Soshichi Miyachi, a TV commentator from Tokyo and chief commentator on the World Business Satellite Program there, will follow. Our next speaker will be Ambassador Seki, the Consul General of Japan in New York, and finally our colleague Professor Paul A. Samuelson will sum it all up and warn us about some things. He said before that it was going to be a little bit of Cassandra today.

MIKE SYNAR

This is a great opportunity for me, and I want to thank New York University and Stern for inviting me to be here. Let me tell you a little bit about myself. I'm a United States Congressman from Oklahoma. I am from Muskogee, Oklahoma. Yes, you've finally met one: An Okie from Muskogee.

My background is that I went to the University of Oklahoma, where I was a triple major in accounting, economics, and finance. I then went to Northwestern University, where I got my masters in management. I spent a year in Edinburgh, Scotland doing post-graduate work in economics at Edinburgh University, and then I came back to the University of Oklahoma and did my law degree in tax specialty. I remember the words of my father as I came off the platform at graduation. He grabbed my hand and said, "Son, you're the most over-educated rancher I've ever met." (My family is a fourth generation ranching family from the State of Oklahoma.)

I went to Congress at the ripe old age of 27. I'm now 42, in my eighth term. My district is a rural area around Tulsa, Oklahoma, and its major products obviously are agricultural products and energy itself. Since going to Washington I've tried to focus my career on issues that are not only vital to Oklahoma, such as agriculture and energy, but also a little bit more global in nature: the issues

46

of environment, as well as the future economic status of our country in this world that is changing so quickly around us.

I gave you that little background because I've come to a conclusion as a congressman from a state that's not necessarily always been in play when we talk about trade. The conclusion is that free trade is good for our country, and free trade is good for all countries. That is why it is so vital as we look at the number of agreements that are going to be considered in the next couple of months that we remember that free trade is a winner for everyone.

I've also come to the conclusion that the NAFTA agreement that is before Congress now is a winner for the United States, a winner for Mexico and Canada, and a winner for the world. As is often the case, however, we have problems selling these trade agreements because too often we lose the opportunity to have a debate based upon the facts. NAFTA and future trade agreements will be heavily laden with politics and fear. As a result, we will find that the issues of protectionism and lack of liberalization will continue to plague us as we sit down at tables seeking bilateral and multilateral types of agreements to try to work these things out.

Understanding what's behind the fear, politics, and protectionism is very important. The political scene is pretty concise. The Republicans who negotiated the NAFTA agreement of years past are uncomfortable with Bill Clinton, not only on this issue but on other issues, and feel very little obligation to champion the agreement they essentially created. The fact is that the Republicans are leaderless now, and for all practical purposes, I say as a Democrat, brain dead. They have relied upon Ross Perot as their head until further notice, and so Ross and his loose facts are dictating many of the marginal Republican theories on this.

Democrats, on the other hand, who did not negotiate the deal, feel some obligation in a new international setting to be the champions of free trade. Yet they're being asked to marry up with a group of businesses and business interests with which they had very little, if any, relationship during the decade of the eighties. In fact they're very uncomfortable with their new partners, given the fact that they are now having to take on base constituencies that have historically been the backbone of the Democratic Party, namely organized labor and working men and women. The fear behind not only NAFTA but other trade agreements really centers on these working men and women of the countries that will be affected.

In our own country, with respect to NAFTA, what we're finding is that we're not really debating the issue of the impact of NAFTA on labor. We're really debating the consequences of what has been for fifteen to twenty years a steady changing of the workplace in the United States. Men and women in the work force, both organized and unorganized, find themselves for the first time having at least some control over the future, their own future as they see it. The eighties to them was a decade where paper chasing took precedence over manufacturing, where corporations became insensitive to job layoffs, where collective bargaining agreements revolved around cutting back on benefits such as health care, and where job security became the driving force behind most negotiations. Lay on top of that this new decade and the new agreements, and working men and women fear that NAFTA is just another stone thrown at them, or another brick that they're going to have to carry. I find myself trying to talk to working men and women in my district and throughout the country on the issue of NAFTA, and very rarely is it the issue of NAFTA at stake. The real fears are a consequence of everything that happened to labor during the decade of the eighties.

Now selling NAFTA or selling any free trade agreement is in my estimation a major marketing job. We have to go around the channels that we would normally use, which are statistical and factual, to deal many times directly with peoples' emotions. I might add to our Japanese friends that some of these recommendations I'm making for my own countrymen could be used in Japan as well. In my travels there I have found that the fears that Japanese Diet members have with respect to dealing with their constituencies closely parallel those in our own country.

First of all we have to convince working men and women in the United States and other countries that are affected by trade agreements that they are good for them in the long run, not only for themselves but for their children. I don't think you can do it through numbers. As you've seen on TV here in New York, both sides have an unlimited advertising budget, and each is claiming that 700,000 jobs will be created or 700,000 jobs will be lost, and somewhere in the middle is the truth.

I was in Mawki, Oklahoma, a town about twenty-five miles south of Tulsa, last year, and I was going through Ball Glass, which is headquartered in Indiana. It employs about 700 people to make the jars and glassware used throughout the marketing of Kraft products. Before my eyes some tiny little jars made their way down the assembly line. They looked like Ken and Barbie Miracle Whip mayonnaise jars. Really small jars.

When we got to the back of the factory and were sitting in the coffee room I asked one of the labor stewards, "What was that going down the assembly line?" He said, "Those were miniature Miracle Whip mayonnaise jars." "Where are they going?" I asked. "They're going to Mexico." I said, "I was told that if NAFTA passed, one of the first industries that would really feel the impact would be the glass industry." "Well, I don't know about that," he said, "but we know we have $30 million worth of contracts over the next ten years right here in this plant. This is going to mean very good employment for our workers."

I asked why the jars are so small, and he said, "Well, there are two separate reasons. First, for the Mexican market all they can afford is that size of Miracle Whip; and second, since refrigeration is not common in Mexico it has to be a one-time use item." I thought to myself that's the kind of innovation, the kind of spirit, the kind of things that have made America a commanding presence in the world market. It has to be repeated over and over again, so that American workers can have confidence that if the rules are fair and level we can compete and win as many battles as we'll lose in this trade war.

So the first thing is selling labor on the idea, and I think the best way to do it is to use examples. For instance, there are many ranchers in my state of Oklahoma who are absolutely convinced that if we sign a NAFTA agreement, the Mexicans will flood the market with cattle and therefore cattle prices will be forced down. If one has ever traveled to Mexico, if one has ever looked at the terrain of Mexico, one has to ask, as I have, where they are going to put all those cattle. They don't have the capacity on their land to do it. Such fear can be alleviated then by a simple description of the situation for our cattlemen using anecdotal information.

The second way to sell free trade agreements for countries like the United States and others is by recognizing the benefits. NAFTA, for example, shows us something that we could preach all over the world. The NAFTA agreement is the first international trade agreement that includes environmental controls. That benefit alone will set precedents obliging all treaties that are being negotiated presently or in the future to include environmental concerns of the planet. That's important, because it creates a constituency for these treaties that you wouldn't naturally have. Trying to emphasize the environmental benefits can help countries bring their constituencies around.

When those who have opposed NAFTA in my own

district, and let me assure you that's about 70 percent, finally get down to the hub of the debate, it comes to this. I look across the table to them and I say, "Describe for me what happens if we don't sign it. Does the environment get better? Are there any rules on health and safety? Is there any tying of wages to productivity? Are there any markets developed? Or do we give unilateral tariff control back over to the Mexicans and the Canadians and our trading partners to a point where we could literally be crushed? Are we willing, if we don't sign NAFTA, to literally turn over probably the second-largest market outside of China to the Japanese and the Germans and the French and others who are already there and prepared to take advantage of it?" These are questions that I think can really take the opposition and ask them for the burden of proof to show the consequences of not moving in that direction.

Another thing I think it is important to understand is something I learned in Japan last August at a conference on "Global Legislatures on a Balanced Environment." Together with a number of other members of Congress and the United States Senate, I met with Japanese, Russian, and European parliamentarians—and came away convinced that in the case of NAFTA, if it fails it will very likely set dominos in motion which could make nationalism and protectionism the order of the day around the world. The United States is the largest market and the largest trading partner. If we can't get our own house in order, if we can't convince our own people of the merits of this free trade agreement, then we will have less leverage on the framework agreement, on GATT, on every agreement we are presently negotiating, both multilateral and bilateral. I think we can sell NAFTA as a necessary basis for the future of all the other trade agreements we have.

Let me conclude my remarks with a prediction. As history has shown, most agreements and most treaties that we've had to deal with in the United States start way behind. Those of you who are old enough to remember the Panama Canal Treaty know that there was a 3 to 1 opposition in the United States upon its introduction, and it barely passed at the end. That seems to be the case now with NAFTA and the other trade agreements that are being negotiated. We started way behind. I think that the opposition to NAFTA peaked about three weeks ago, and we have steadily made progress in a number of areas in moving members of the House of Representatives from no to undecided, and some from undecided into the yes category.

We are scheduled to vote on NAFTA on the floor of the House of Representatives on November 17, 1993, and if it passes the House then on November 18 it will go to the Senate. I don't think it's going to pass by more than five votes. It will require Republicans to overwhelmingly support it, and Democrats who presently are not supporting it to put up some numbers that would represent nearly half the caucus of the Democratic party. I also predict that what happens on November 17 and 18 will have long-term implications on a variety of fronts, whether Japanese-United States relationships, GATT, or anything else. In less than a month then, in fact a month to the day, we as Americans, and we who view these world trade agreements as important parts of the future of the world, will have a pretty good blueprint of what the future of trade protectionism and liberalization is all about.

ROBERT KAVESH: North America is not the only place in the world where moves toward trade liberalization and market openings are occurring. Japan is another. We're fortunate today to have Soshichi Miyachi, a major TV commentator in Japan, an expert in macroeconomics and international economic policy, and the author of nine books. He is going to speak on deregulation and market opening in the Japanese economy.

SOSHICHI MIYACHI

My topic for today has to do with the new Japanese administration, the first in thirty-eight years that is not LDP (Liberal Democratic Party). Specifically I would like to touch upon deregulation, one of the focal points of the new administration. I feel that the issue of deregulation in Japan has important implications for the world economy.

Mike Synar will probably agree with me that in the United States a lot of people start their presentations with a joke. I was thinking about a joke that I could begin my presentation with, but I couldn't come up with anything. I feel there is some fairly dark humor, however, inherent in the strange and complex regulatory system that Japanese bureaucrats have created in our country.

As an ombudsman for the Japanese government at the Office of Trade and Investment, I have served for six years on a special grievance resolution group. Our function is to resolve complaints from foreigners who have run into regulatory problems trying to sell their products in Japan. It is clear that we have to make some new laws in our country, and by sharing a few of my personal experiences with our current restrictions I hope to give you a better understanding of what it is we are trying to change.

A Belgian wallpaper company came to us with a complaint concerning Japanese safety standards. The Japanese standards are based upon a test in which the wallpaper is set on fire and the amount of smoke generated by the fire is observed. Belgian safety standards are based upon the EU code. They set fire to a piece of wallpaper and they look at how fast it burns. Although the wallpaper in question had met the European standards, the Belgian company was prohibited from selling their product in Japan because they had not submitted it to the Japanese safety test. Since the Japanese test pretty much follows the lines of "where there's smoke there's fire" we felt the European test was equivalent, and we recommended that the Ministry of Construction, which has jurisdiction over this regulation, should permit the product to be imported.

The Ministry of Construction referred us to the Civil Inspection Association, which is directly responsible for performing the safety tests. When we contacted it we discovered the true nature of the problem. The Association was in essence a group of insiders from Japanese industry backed by the Ministry of Construction, and anyone who wanted to become a member from the outside had to pay exorbitant fees. It was extremely difficult in fact for an outside company to become a member of the association or even to get its products tested. So these regulations basically hindered private initiative, and at the same time served to protect a Japanese domestic industry.

Another example of the way our regulatory system works relates to Japanese supermarkets. They sell food, prepared food, that you can buy and take home with you. If, however, the preparation of that food was done outside the supermarket, each and every one of the specific kitchens in which the food was prepared would have to be authorized separately. You also need a separate license to sell milk products. This, I believe, is simply overintervention on the part of the Japanese bureaucracy.

It should be noted at this point that Japanese industrial policies have certainly not affected all industries in the same way. When we consider the protection of domestic industry in Japan some characteristics seem to recur repeatedly, but at the same time striking differences can be seen when each industry is considered individually. The auto industry, for instance, is somewhat of an exception to the rule in Japan. For one thing no laws have been specifically drafted pertaining to the Japanese auto industry, although high tariffs do protect the Japanese market to a certain extent. Japanese auto makers have historically competed fiercely in and among themselves, but when necessary they have also been able to cooperate with each other. The Japanese electronics industry and the assembly industry in general, on the other hand, appear to have benefited considerably by the multitude of regulations which specifically govern their operations.

The Hosokawa administration is trying to place deregulation at the top of the list of priorities for economic policy, and I personally hope and pray that this will proceed. If it does, I believe it will contribute greatly to the changes that are occurring throughout the Japanese economy and the Japanese market mechanism. At the same time, however, I have some doubts. The Japanese economy is very weak at the moment. To be more specific, in

1992 the Japanese economy grew in real terms at a rate of 0.8 percent. If we take national income into account, we may actually be looking at a negative growth rate. Deregulation, even if it is pursued, is not going to give Japanese industry the capability to absorb the kinds of costs that are going to be required to adjust successfully to the fluctuations in our economy.

Compared with the last quarter of fiscal 1993 (October to December), real growth rates will probably be about 0.3 percent from January to March of 1994. If those levels are achieved there will be zero growth in the Japanese marketplace, which means that there has to have been negative growth before. We have started looking ahead to fiscal 1994, and right now the estimates are somewhere along the lines of 1 percent. Even level growth is based on a sudden recovery, or an assumption of sudden recovery, in the latter half of fiscal 1994.

According to my recollection, during his first administration President Reagan conducted very large-scale deregulation. At the same time, however, he introduced a major reduction in taxes. He stimulated personal consumption in this way in order to stimulate the American economy as a whole. It was the reduction in taxes together with deregulation that brought about the boom in the Reagan years, I believe. In looking only at deregulation, without the tax reform component, the Hosokawa administration is setting aside the most important aspect of Ronald Reagan's strategy. I am concerned therefore about resistance within the Japanese economy toward the proposed deregulation.

In any consideration of deregulation, it is important to have some perspective on the bureaucracy that came up with all these regulations in the first place. After World War II Japan needed to strengthen its international competitiveness. Developing apace with the general growth of the Japanese economy, the bureaucracy naturally introduced industrial policies with that purpose in mind. Intended to present a barrier to any new entry into the marketplace, the regulations tended to be oligopolistic by their very nature.

In effect an "iron triangle" was forged of politics, bureaucracy, and business, fortified by the varied succession of laws and regulations that were promulgated through the postwar years. The regulatory policy that developed as a result of these laws, however, has created obstacles for Japanese private industry as often as it has served to protect that industry. The question of how to dismantle the triangle is a major problem now in Japan and lies at the heart of the political debate.

One way to bring about the results we seek would involve changing the very structures by which government and industry in Japan relate to each other. Japanese bureaucrats often provide basic administrative guidance to industries, and we will need to revise our domestic laws to change or eliminate this practice. The Bush administration pointed out the need to establish some kind of dialogue to begin to accomplish this, and such a dialogue has in fact begun with the Structural Impediment Initiatives (SII). As a result of the SII talks, several Japanese laws have in fact already been revised.

Our antimonopoly act, for instance, has been called the least enforced law in the world, and tightening it up has been one of the priorities of the Hosokawa administration. I believe that in the short run the administration will be unsuccessful in this goal, simply because there was such a lack of enforcement in the past. However, penalties have been increased and the Japanese commercial code itself has been strengthened to more closely resemble the American code. As the Bush administration did before him, although his methods and style are different, I believe President Clinton will continue to attempt to influence the direction of Japanese industrial policy by pushing for the revision of more domestic laws in the future.

ROBERT KAVESH: Ambassador Hiromoto Seki, Consul General of Japan in New York, has been a diplomat for most of his career. In this capacity he has had a chance to see a great deal of the world, and he's going to speak to us next about Japanese policy making in general.

HIROMOTO SEKI

The subject of today's discussion, "Trade Negotiations and Agreements: A Trend toward Further Liberalization," is very pertinent to the events of the day. I believe that the negotiations and agreements being worked out now to liberalize trade will ultimately enable all the parties involved to enjoy the benefits of economic interchange on a global scale.

The Uruguay Round of the GATT is one of the most important of the current negotiations relating to global trade. Japan, with the cooperation of its trading partners, is working hard for its successful conclusion. This past July, the participants at the Tokyo Summit—Canada, the European Union, the United States, and Japan—issued a joint statement reaffirming their determination to build a free trade system and to conclude the Uruguay Round by the end of this year. The statement called for the complete elimination of tariffs on an extensive list of products that included pharmaceuticals, construction equipment, medical equipment, furniture, farm equipment, and spirits. I believe that this kind of agreement will significantly promote the successful conclusion of the Uruguay Round.

At the same time as the Tokyo Summit, but separately, President Clinton and then Prime Minister Miyazawa were announcing the framework for a new economic partnership between Japan and the United States. Their meeting reflected a serious commitment by both countries to ironing out problems in their trade relationship. They have provided a structure for ongoing consultations, including biannual meetings of the heads of the governments, with the goal of substantially increasing access and sales of competitive foreign goods and services in both countries through market opening and other economic measures; increasing investment; promoting international competitiveness; and enhancing bilateral economic cooperation.

Under the terms of this agreement, Japan will actively pursue the objectives of promoting strong and substantial demand, and increasing market access to competitive foreign goods and services. Japan intends to achieve a highly significant decrease in its current account surplus and to promote a significant increase in global imports of goods and services, including, of course, those from the United States. The United States in turn will pursue the objective of substantially reducing its budget deficit by promoting domestic savings and strengthening its international competitiveness.

Although the framework does mention sets of objective trade criteria, it was not intended to include numerical targets. Setting numerical targets is a bad idea for many reasons. For one thing it is based upon a false premise, because the Japanese government could not control the activities of Japanese companies even if we wanted it to. Second, by setting numerical targets one is trying to manage trade. Why would anyone want to encourage this kind of government control over economic activities? Third, numerical targets would hurt rather than support American competitiveness. If you guarantee a share of the market to American companies, it means certain companies will be selectively rewarded whether they produce high-quality products or not. This is clearly not in America's best interest.

I believe the most important argument against numerical targets, however, was the one laid out in an open letter in 1993 to President Clinton and Prime Minister Hosokawa by over 30 leading economists, including four Nobel Laureates. One of them, Professor Paul A. Samuelson, is with us on this panel today. These eminent economists all believe that numerical targets would harm Japan-U.S. trade relations and the entire world trading system.

A more positive effort to reduce Japan's trade surplus was the announcement by the Hosokawa administration on September 16, 1993, just one month ago, of its third economic package to be unveiled in the past thirteen months. It is a substantial effort to rekindle the economy. Calling for over ¥6 trillion in government spending, the plan includes wide sweeping measures to deregulate the economy. The 94 items of deregulation will have a direct impact on the expansion of domestic demand and the promotion of imports, and should thereby help Japan fulfill its obligation to the balance of trade. As Miyachi warned earlier, the efforts for deregulation in Japan, although a step in the right direction, may encounter opposition. I certainly hope, as a consumer myself in Japanese society, that the efforts for deregulation will prevail over any bureaucratic or other opposition that may exist in Japan and will have a very serious impact upon the functioning of the Japanese economy.

The new administration of Prime Minister Hosokawa has pledged to bring about political, economic, and administrative reform. His proposed economic measures show definite progress in the right direction. The most recent committee appointed to come up with a plan for economic reform will release a report in the near future outlining further steps to be taken. The end result should be a more open system that is beneficial to consumers, and a more positive contribution by Japan overall to the world trading system.

It might be hard to imagine just how serious Japan's current recession is, and why these reforms are so necessary. Let me give you some examples:

During the past three years Japan's stock market fell at one time over 60 percent. Despite slowly recovery, it is still only at 56 percent of its highest level. The residential real estate market plummeted 50 percent in two years; industrial production dropped over 8 percent in one year; and corporate bankruptcy has tripled since 1990. It is estimated that roughly 7 to 8 trillion dollars' worth of asset values, a figure about 20 to 30 percent larger than the U.S. annual GNP, has been eliminated by these declines. As a result, the recession has had a direct impact on the volume of Japanese imports.

American exports to Japan increased annually by 13

percent from 1985, the year of the Plaza Accord, until 1991—the largest increase in foreign exports that the United States has ever experienced with any country. Only in 1992 did they record a modest decrease (0.8 percent). Coupled with America's import growth of 6.2 percent, reflecting the beginning of economic recovery in this country, the trade imbalance widened. Japan's recession therefore has had a clear impact on the trade balance. Prime Minister Hosokawa's economic package, through expansion and deregulation, takes sure steps in the direction of recovery.

I'd like to make an important point about America's trade deficit with Japan. The numbers can be somewhat misleading. For example, measured in dollar terms we see an increase in the trade imbalance during the second quarter of 1992 as compared to the second quarter of 1993. However, when measured in yen there is a decrease in trade imbalance when comparing these two periods. Japanese global exports have already started to decline in yen terms in recent months. It is crucial to study these facts.

NAFTA is currently the most talked about issue in the United States. Since NAFTA has already become one of the most controversial domestic issues in American politics, however, I am hesitant to express my personal views on it. I only hope that NAFTA advocates will not overly emphasize the merits of creating an exclusive trading block for the North American Continent. At the same time I hope its opponents will not give an overly distorted view of possible industrial dislocation by NAFTA, as if any free international trade would be bound to harm the American economy.

I feel that the United States should pay greater attention to the Asia Pacific region. In 1991 the Asia Pacific region accounted for 51 percent of world GNP, twice the percentage for the European Union. As President Clinton said in a recent speech at Waseda University in Tokyo, over 40 percent of American trade is currently with this region. Last year over 2.3 million American jobs were created as a result of the $120 billion exported to Asia.

In November 1993, Seattle will host an important event in Asia Pacific history. We will witness not only the Fifth Annual Ministry Meeting, but the first heads of state meeting of the Asia Pacific Economic Corporation, or APEC. This is a forum for Asian and Pacific countries to bring their minds together to formulate regional cooperation so as to further accelerate this dynamic region's economy. I hope APEC will be able to utilize this epoch-making occasion to promote trade expansion within our region, but even more importantly to encourage global trading expansion and economic integration. I certainly hope that this historic event will remind America of the ever-increasing potential of the Asia Pacific region for the United States, which is after all one of the leading nations of the global community.

ROBERT KAVESH: I give you our final speaker for the day, Professor Paul A. Samuelson. When I was a student in college I learned my economics from the fourth edition of Professor Samuelson's textbook on economics, and I think he told us this morning the fifteenth edition is about to come out. It must be one of the great best-sellers of all time.

PAUL A. SAMUELSON

President Clinton began 1993 with bad luck in the realm of international economics. America's balance of payments deficit has been getting worse rather than better. This is a serious blow to his political popularity, and a potential threat to his reelection in 1996.

An important reason that Candidate Clinton defeated George Bush was his promise to the voters to create good new jobs to replace those being lost at IBM, General Motors, Proctor & Gamble, and everywhere among large and small American corporations. So where have the good jobs gone? Advanced technology has not been lost on this continent. Those good jobs can be said to have largely gone abroad where they can be performed by lower-paid labor working with footloose knowledge and equipment—first to the EU, then later to the Pacific Basin.

American exports to Latin America began the year strong. We have been running a sizable surplus with Mexico, for example. The new Clinton team had hoped that the Japanese and German locomotives would come to life and join in with our recovery effort, thereby improving our exports to them too.

The economists on the Clinton team are, for the most part, advocates of free trade. At the Council of Economic Advisers I have in mind in qualified degree Laura Tyson and in less qualified degree Alan Blinder and Joseph Stiglitz; and at the Treasury and in the White House, economists such as Undersecretary Lawrence Summers and Dr. David Cutler. Surely they must be very disappointed that Europe and Japan remain in the doldrums. When unemployment grows in those countries and spendable incomes stagnate, their citizenry cut down on imports from America. No wonder Japan's bilateral balance of trade with America reaches new record levels. And this happens despite depreciation of the dollar relative to the yen, in a vicious cumulative downward spiral whose end is not yet in sight.

Politically, this is storing up trouble for Japan. Trouble may also spill over for Korea, Taiwan, Singapore, Hong Kong, and also for the European Union. Americans on Main Street are turning impatient. In Congress those of both political parties are being tempted in the direction of protectionism. I see a danger that the President himself may revert back toward the foreigner-bashing he had been recently talked out of by his economic advisers. Mr. Clinton may even lose the congressional vote on ratification of the NAFTA free trade treaty between the U.S., Mexico, and Canada. Even America's signing off on the Uruguay Round of GATT multilateralism can still be said to be problematic.

This means that the pro-protectionism advisers who were so important in the early Clinton presidential campaign—Robert Reich, Secretary of Labor; Ron Brown, Secretary of Commerce; Ira Magaziner; and always to be suspected Wall Street investment bankers such as Treasury

Deputy Secretary Roger Altman and White House National Economic Council Chairman Robert Rubens—may revert back toward a get-tougher economic policy.

I shall not be surprised if we begin to hear even more about managed trade. If it becomes popular to give Japan an ultimatum to accept more American exports while exporting less themselves to America, why stop with Japan? Why not a new shopping list with specific requests addressed toward Korea and the other Small Dragons? Why not tough talk and threats directed toward Spain, Italy, and Europe generally?

Not all the developing countries are equally vulnerable to political pressures. Chile, Brazil, Argentina, and Mexico are not in the same boat with China. When China under "market socialism" grows at 12 percent per year, much of its energy comes from cheap exports to America. The shoes I wear, the clothing on my back, my inexpensive radio and new tennis racket increasingly bear the label "Made in China." The China-U.S. trade surplus is soaring up toward Japan-U.S. magnitude. That makes China vulnerable in a way that Mexico is not.

There is a moral in this for South Korea. Just as Japan has been learning the hard way that in her own self-interest she ought not continue to rely principally on export-led growth, the EC countries would be well advised to use the freedoms gained after the breakdown of the pegged exchange rate system to initiate monetary and fiscal stimulus measures.

I doubt that President Clinton will score great successes

in his export drives. All the more reason to fear that future policy will be tempted to veer in the direction of what comes politically easy—namely new initiatives to clamp down on imports into the United States.

People abroad should be praying that America's recovery will turn more vigorous. Experience during the post-1982 years of Reagan and Bush showed that what kept political protectionism in check was American prosperity at home. New jobs, even if many of them were not high-paying manufacturing jobs, took the edge off American voter discontent, reducing the pressures on congressional legislators to agitate for protectionism.

Ross Perot, the populist multibillionaire, was kept out of office in the 1992 election campaign. He did not succeed in getting a plurality of the votes. Perot, however, remains in active politics. He conducts public meetings. He spends his own money to buy television time to present criticisms of President Clinton's proposals.

I have a friend who is a Texas millionaire and a friend of Ross Perot's. When Perot announced for the Presidency, my friend said to him: "Ross, why don't you get the best economist in the world for your adviser?" "Who would that be, Tom?" "I mean Paul Samuelson." "Samuelson? Isn't that the guy who believes in the law of comparative advantage? That's just a theory in my book." I told my friend Tom Marsh, "Next time don't send me the business."

Perot is a protectionist through and through. He claims that free trade with Mexico will kill off a million American jobs. If elected to the Presidency, he can be expected to turn hostile to competition from abroad. If the going gets rough for William Clinton, in self-defense he might himself be forced into a protectionist direction, even if that is not in America's long-run self-interest. I hope I am wrong in this fear.

CHAPTER 3

International Competitiveness In High-Technology Industries

December 8, 1993

INTRODUCTORY REMARKS

ROBERT KAVESH: They used to say about French generals that they were experts in fighting wars that had taken place earlier, which is in part why the French have rarely won over the last 125 years. Today's topic relates both to academia and to the industrial world. I picked up the latest copy of *Newsweek* and here is this huge article, "Japan Incorporated: Rest in Peace." It contains a detailed introduction to the topic (the Nikkei rollercoaster), along with little sections dealing with what might be called major news items of the past decade or so. Here, in 1985, is Lee Iacocca saying, "It's not Russia that's laying waste to my business, it's Japan, our friend." A little later on, in 1988, "U.S. law makers bash Toshiba radios with sledgehammers after it is learned that the company sold submarine technology to the Soviet Union." From early 1992 comes one of the most famous pictures we've experienced or seen of President Bush, treating Prime Minister Miyazawa to a hot meal.

The article discusses the current difficulties in Japan, and we've all read about them. Down and down and down. Japan's share of the U.S. car market plunges. The pendulum swings back and forth. A propos today's topic, Japan is losing her lead in high technology.

In any event, our topic is "International Competitiveness in High-Technology Industries." Our first speaker is

75

Sadahei Kusumoto, Chairman of Minolta Corporation. Before the meeting we had a chat about living in the United States and matters of that sort. I told him that I am the proud owner of a Minolta camera, which enables me, a klutz with things like that, to take excellent pictures. Following Mr. Kusumoto is Thomas Pugel, a colleague of mine and Chairman of the Department of International Business here at the school. Lastly, Paul A. Samuelson: Friend of the University, Long-Term Credit Bank of Japan Visiting Professor of Political Economy for several years and the first American Nobel Laureate in Economics. We'll see what happens.

SADAHEI KUSUMOTO

I would first like to talk specifically about Minolta, and then to address more general trends within the Japanese electronics industry. Most people know Minolta as a camera company. Yes, we spend almost 80 percent of our advertising budget on camera products, because it's a consumer product. People know Minolta as a camera company. But at this moment only 30 percent of our revenue comes from camera products. The other 70 percent comes from business equipment, mostly copy machines, facsimiles, document image systems, and laser printers. This part of our business has been growing by 10 to 15 percent every year, even over the last three difficult years.

At the same time, however, the camera business is shrinking; electronics is beginning to take over our industry. People who were in New York in the 1950s or early 1960s may remember the display windows of camera stores divided 50 percent for still cameras and another 50 percent for movie cameras. They had movie cameras by Keystone, Bell and Howell, DeJur, and so many others. But you won't find any more movie cameras. They've been completely displaced by video. The same thing may happen soon in the rest of the camera industry, which is why Eastman/Kodak is trying to get into the compact disc business. We know we have to go in this direction as well, for the still camera may very well go the way of the eight millimeter movie camera.

Accordingly, about eighteen months ago there was an announcement by Eastman/Kodak, Canon, Minolta, Nikon, and Fuji Film that we are all going to change our format in the near future. (Because of antitrust laws, we had to make this announcement far in advance.) The new format falls somewhere between conventional and electronic photography. Using existing film, the new magazine is designed to hook up easily with a television and a converter so you will be able to see the image both on TV and in printed format. That's the way we're going.

So electronics is going to play a very important part in our camera business, and of course in the business equipment field electronics is already a major part of our business. When you open a copier or facsimile machine, you will find that 99 percent of the parts were made by other electronics companies. We always joke about it. We're selling a Minolta copy machine, but actually we're selling parts from Toshiba, Hitachi, Sanyo, and Sharp. We just put them together and stamp on the Minolta name. We're the biggest customer for other electronics companies.

Over the past twenty years Japanese companies did very well in stand-alone consumer electronics, from tape recorders to televisions and finally camcorders. But this success is fading out. We are hearing more and more about multifunctional products. Video computers, facsimiles, and telephones can now be united in one product working smoothly together like an orchestra, and up until now Japan has not been prepared to deal with this multimedia trend.

The world of multimedia was introduced in 1989 at a convention sponsored by Bill Gates of Microsoft at Makuhari in Tokyo. It was a sensation for the electronics industry, including the business equipment industry. This multimedia convention has become one of the biggest events of its kind in Japan, because everybody knows this is the way the electronics industry, or even the business equipment industry, is going to end up.

When I originally drafted this speech I spent two pages on the role of the Japanese government, because these multifunctional devices can never succeed in Japan as long as we have so many restrictive laws and regulations. Our industries are controlled both by MITI, the Ministry of International Trade and Industry, and by the Postal and Telecommunications Bureau. These two bureaus never get along. They fight each other for a share of the business. I was planning to explain what kind of obstacles we face before we can embark on the new superhighway of multimedia. Then, on December 3, just five days ago, the powerful Postal and Telecommunications Bureau announced they are going to change that route completely.

Up to now any foreign company, specifically any American company, could invest in no more than 20 percent of Japanese cable TV corporations. According to their recent statement, however, the Postal and Telecommunications

Bureau is going to abandon this 20 percent limit. In other words, anyone interested in getting into the Japanese multimedia business can do so. This is a very unusual step for the Japanese government to take. As you know, the Japanese government is very protective of our industries.

The United States is far ahead in the multimedia business. If you go to Tokyo, you can listen to only three channels of FM radio. From twenty to a hundred radio stations can exist in one place, but because of regulations, sometimes politically motivated, you can only get three channels. Cable television is almost non-existent at this moment in Japan. When the new multifunctional device becomes the mainstream of the electronics industry Japan is going to be left way behind, and our government has finally begun to realize how much help we are going to need from America. Hence, the loosening of regulations.

Of course we have another problem in Japan quite apart from government regulation: Keiretsu, or group-oriented business. After the war, the Japanese banks played a major role in rebuilding and in fact reshaping industry. At a time when everyone needed money desperately the banks lent heavily—but only to manufacturers, who could use their factories as collateral. Unable to borrow from the banks, retail dealers and distributors turned to their manufacturers for financing. Companies like Mitsubishi, Mitsui, and Fuji began to form powerful groups forged together by strong loyalty from the dealers and distributors, who could not, after all, have survived without their help. These loyalties continue to the present day. It is no wonder that an American company would find it difficult to break into the Japanese marketplace, where most dealers are still pledged to one of the major manufacturing groups. Even within the borders of Japan itself these groups compete fiercely with each other, often making it difficult even for Japanese companies to do business within another group's territory.

Minolta is located in Osaka, and we do very well there with all our products. Our cameras, purchased by individual consumers, do well anywhere they are sold. When we try to sell our copy machines outside of Osaka, however, we run into problems. We rely on companies, not consumers, to purchase our business equipment—and you can be sure that these companies are going to belong to some kind of keiretsu (or group). So unless we have strong friends in Tokyo, we are going to encounter difficulty selling our products there.

You may be familiar with another area dominated by this phenomenon of keiretsu, the Japanese auto industry. From assembly line to parts suppliers each group functions as a force unto itself, unified, strong, and highly competitive. This way of operating is a far cry from the kind of cooperation and interdependence required by a computer company to work together with diverse electronics or even camera companies. Sometimes the walls between the keiretsu can bend the core corporations themselves, and I think Japanese industry is going to face this problem in the very near future.

Clearly Japan dominated the electronics industry over the past 20 years. But as far as I can see, the United States has picked up the lead for at least the next decade. How fast Japan can catch up remains a big question.

THOMAS PUGEL

I would like to follow up on Kusumotosan's remarks. He has focused rather noticeably on electronics, and on what I would consider to be the systems-products end of the industry. I'd like to shift now to the components end, the various little things that he said went into that product that eventually had a Minolta name stamped on it. Specifically I'd like to talk about the semiconductor industry, an industry that I've been researching in one way or another for well over a decade now.

Semiconductors are clearly a key technology product with pervasive applications into all sorts of things—consumer products, industrial products, and defense products. It's an industry that exhibits very rapid growth in terms of its sales volume. For instance, in 1992 worldwide sales of semiconductors rose by about 20 percent, and they are expected to rise again this year by about 20 percent. That's a little bit above but pretty close to the long-term trend for the industry—a very rapid-growth, fast-moving industry.

Let's look back to the early 1980s and review some comments you have already heard. There were substantial concerns about the future of the U.S. industry. U.S. firms' share of the world's merchant semiconductor market was falling from about 60 percent to about 40 percent in the space of six years, roughly 1980 to 1986. Japanese firms' share of worldwide semiconductor sales was rising almost in step, 30 percent up to about 46 percent. Thus the Japanese industry as a whole became the single largest national industry in that sector. Japanese firms' gains were mainly in memory-integrated circuits, and especially in a product known as DRAMs (Dynamic Random Access Memory). Looking at it from a national level, the U.S. share of the Japanese market had remained rather steady at what U.S. firms considered to be an unfortunately and unacceptably low level of about 10 percent from the early 1970s, well into the mid-1980s.

That led to some substantial trade friction. U.S. firms complained in the mid-1980s that Japanese firms were dumping both DRAMs and another memory product, EPROMS (Erasable Programmable Read Only Memory). The U.S. firms charged and sued on the basis that Japanese firms were infringing on various patented U.S. technology. U.S. firms complained to our government that there were obstacles to accessing the Japanese market based less on formal barriers from the past, which had essentially all been removed by the mid seventies, than on the various trading, dealing, and supplier/buyer relationships just described by Kusumoto—the keiretsu.

As the U.S. firms put it, a market structure existed that was conducive to reciprocal dealing and that effectively excluded outsiders, including outsiders from elsewhere in Japan. There was alleged pressure to buy Japanese, and the government certainly supported various kinds of research and development projects, cooperative projects within Japan. The U.S. firms also alleged that Japanese firms were engaging in "capacity-expansion races," races based on trying to gain larger market shares. Of course that's a zero-sum game, a very dangerous game to try to play if everyone's playing the same way. It led to periodic overcapacity, and a tendency for Japanese firms to engage in the dumping that we mentioned earlier.

Japanese firms disputed all these charges, claiming misinterpretation by the Americans of various aspects of Japanese business. Out of all of this conflict, however, came a 1986 agreement in which the Japanese government committed to encouraging the purchase of foreign semiconductors in Japan. Although not part of the formal agreement at this point, there was even a side letter where the Japanese government acknowledged the notion of a 20 percent share by 1991 for foreign semiconductors, somewhat more than doubling the share that existed in 1986. That agreement also put in place a cost-price monitoring system for Japanese exports.

In 1987 the U.S. government imposed sanctions, 100 percent tariffs on a variety of non-semiconductor products, based on the failure of the Japanese government to prevent dumping out of Japan, and the failure of the Japanese government to enhance market access into Japan. The dumping sanctions were removed later that year when the dumping ended, driven mainly by strong market growth. Also in 1987 U.S. industry formed a consortium known as Sematech, which received half of its funding, about $100 million a year, from the U.S. government, and half from the private consortium members. The goal was to develop state-of-the-art production techniques.

When the 1986 semiconductor agreement expired in 1991, it was renewed for another five years. This time the goal of a 20 percent foreign share of the Japanese market was formally included in the agreement, to be achieved by the end of 1992. Thereafter a gradual and steady improvement in market access was supposed to take place. Also included in that agreement was continued monitoring of export prices. As part of the process, the remaining sanctions from 1987 were lifted.

What we see as we move into the present is an immense number of private decisions made and actions taken by firms in the United States, as well as a variety of actions taken by the U.S. government; intriguingly, these governmental actions were instituted during the Reagan administration. This is Reagan's industrial policy at work. Equally intriguing from my point of view, these various actions seem to have been reasonably effective, with better results in fact than I would have ever expected. Government policies did not seem to hurt things, and in many ways seem to have contributed to what now looks to be really a quite good performance by U.S. industry. U.S. firms' share of the world market continued to fall to 37 percent in 1989 but then began rising back, and we are now at more than 40 percent. We have had in fact a four-year upward trend in the U.S. share of the world market for semiconductors, while Japanese firms' shares have fallen from about 50 percent to about 43 percent.

Foreign shares of the Japanese market were 8.6 percent in the third quarter of 1986, when the first agreement was signed. They hit a level of 14 to 16 percent during 1991 and most of 1992. Then, remarkably, and to the surprise of almost everyone, the foreign firms' share of the Japanese market hit 20.2 percent in the fourth quarter of 1992. Some of that rise was due to last-ditch efforts by the Japanese firms. I was somewhat disheartened actually to see that Kusumoto's list of the ingredients in Minolta's products did not include any mention of components by Texas Instruments or Intel. Perhaps it was just an oversight. At any rate, Japanese purchases of foreign, mainly U.S., semiconductors in that fourth quarter rose by 8 percent, even as overall market sales within Japan were declining. Put that together and you've got a 20.2 percent market share.

For the first half of 1993, the foreign market share continues to run between 19 and 20 percent. This doesn't seem to be just a one-quarter fluke. Something has happened here, and I think arguably this would not have happened without that 1986 agreement in place. U.S. firms' shares might have risen anyway, but not by this much. An agreement about semiconductors appears to have succeeded in altering some deeply entrenched behavior connected to the buyer/supplier relationship in Japan.

Related to this scenario is concern in the United States about our firms' production of the equipment that makes semiconductors: chip-making equipment. The U.S. share of the world market for chip-making equipment has also recently been rising, and it's back up above 40 percent. Industry sources here generally credit Sematech with some of that advance. Sematech sounds like a project to produce semiconductors, but it's really a project involved in trying to enhance the capabilities in producing production technology. That mainly means process machines, substantial support being offered to U.S. production of the chip-making equipment. That's part of the picture. The other part of the picture is clearly private decisions by U.S. firms, and right now they look to have pulled off the question of product positioning extremely well.

U.S. firms generally have not returned to the production of memory-integrated circuits, however. The DRAMs especially are not something that have pulled U.S. firms back into production. In that sense you might judge the 1986 agreement to be something of a failure, despite the controls on dumping. Arguably, however, not producing memory-integrated circuits was a very wise decision. Although high in volume, memory-integrated circuits are often low or no or negative margin products. They are commodity products, intensely competitive in nature. In fact Japanese firms are probably paying a price for emphasizing them in terms of not getting the kind of payoffs from their semiconductor investment that they might have expected. One reason for this was at least moderately predictable even by the mid eighties. Any country that's going to go into advanced integrated circuits is going to follow the same path that the Japanese used. They're going to push into those memory ICs. Most notably, Korean firms have been doing just that.

Korean firms have gained 25 percent of the world market for DRAMs. Japanese share is now down to about 55 percent. How did the Koreans do it? The formula sounds familiar: A low price strategy, subsidy by government loans and government research projects for basic production technologies, with licensing of technology where necessary from foreign firms. That competitive thrust by the Koreans is hitting the Japanese firms head on in a product area where the Japanese had been the dominant players. Yet the overall share of Korean firms in the world market is only 4 percent. Outside of DRAMs they are minor players, and they have not had much effect on the general U.S. semiconductor business.

History repeats itself yet again. A small U.S. firm, Micron, which is focused on DRAM production, filed a dumping suit against the Korean firms late last year. The Korean firms were found guilty of dumping, although the punitive duties imposed by the Commerce Department were relatively small. Potentially they could have been astronomical. One firm was hit with preliminary dumping duties of 87 percent, which would have effectively shut them out of the U.S. market. In the final determination, however, the duties were lowered. Some firms were hit with dumping duties of less than 1 percent, which is trivial, hardly enough to even influence behavior; others were hit as high as 11½ percent.

This outcome has helped Micron. It helps the Japanese firms, which are going to feel a little less price pressure from the Korean competition. It harms, at least a little, all of the other U.S. firms that are attempting to use these products. As I have argued for a long time, applying dumping laws to this industry is an extremely dicey business. First of all, it is difficult to measure whether dumping actually exists in any meaningful sense. Furthermore, potential losses to user industries are far more likely than any gains to U.S. producers. In this case only one small U.S. producer seems likely to have benefited in any real way. Texas Instruments is also in this market area, as is Motorola, but they are basically producing in Japan.

So what are the U.S. firms doing? Well, as they moved into the mid-1980s they became very successful in high-value, high-margin, innovation-driven product areas. This was basically the result of private decision making and strategy at its best. U.S. firms now emphasize application-specific integrated circuits, and they have been fairly successful at holding their own in that market despite competition from the Japanese.

Where the U.S. firms clearly shine is in microprocessors. If you wanted to be in a product area right now, you'd want to be in Intel's business. Intel is now the world's largest semiconductor producer as of 1992. Ninety percent of the world's PCs use Intel microprocessors. It's a nice business, highly profitable. Manufacturing costs for a 486 chip run less than $30.00. The chip sells for about $300.00. That is a recent comparison. Intel's after-tax profit margin on sales last year was 26 percent. The other major microprocessor producers in the world market are basically American as well, Motorola being the other notable one in supplying, among other things, the Apple line of PCs.

A reversal of sorts is flash memory, an important new memory-integrated circuit. Toshiba invented it, but Intel dominates the market—85 percent Intel. Toshiba is scrambling to try to catch up, having ignored the product area and focused on other things.

U.S. firms are also guarding and exploiting their proprietary technology more carefully than before. They see where their strength lies, and they have become more aggressive. Intel's approach is to refuse to license anybody, and to sue anybody who thinks they're going to try to horn in on their microprocessor business. Texas Instruments uses a somewhat different approach, licensing its patents to obtain substantial royalties. A large part of TI's profits come from this patent royalty income. These two different strategies are probably appropriate to each of the individual firms, given their other circumstances.

What we see here is a rather surprising success story. U.S. firm share of the world market has certainly stabilized, perhaps it's even on the up tick. More important, U.S. firms are positioned into what appears to be the better parts of the market—the better parts, the more innovative parts, the parts with higher margins, more profits.

Mainly I think that is the result of private decision

making, private actions by U.S. firms, including some key strategic decisions. Intriguingly, however, there is also a role here for U.S. government policy. U.S. policies have had some positive impact to be sure, although proving that would be extremely difficult. We would have to do a sort of counterfactual removing of all those policies, and I doubt we really have the economic tools to pull that off. But a remarkable piece of Reagan-instituted industrial policy actually seems to have had some positive impact on the industry, especially in the area of market access into Japan in the area of semiconductor equipment manufacturing. There are still some major challenges here for all involved, and I don't want to call the game over. I don't want to declare Japan to be "RIP." I think that would be confusing a cycle with a cyclical movement, and I hesitate to do that.

This is an industry with rapidly rising development and facilities costs, a major challenge to everyone in the industry. A new state-of-the art integrated circuit production facility costs about $1 billion for one factory. Development costs for a new generation of a product, separate from the facilities, also run about $1 billion. Huge investments are going to be needed here. One major private response is the increasing use of alliances, including some major international ones. Using the triad approach, an IBM/Toshiba/Siemens alliance was announced in the last year or so for the purpose of developing 256M DRAMs. We're talking about 10,000 pages of typed text contained in one little chip. Currently the 4M is mainstream, while the 16M chip is in production. So they're looking two generations ahead, assuming an increase by a factor of four.

I have tried to give some specific examples of the notion that in many ways the race for technology is becoming a lot more interesting and competitive. U.S. efforts seem to be paying off with some reasonable results both from government policy and from the private sector.

PAUL A. SAMUELSON

Economic theory does not claim that a healthy economy can be "competitive" in all goods and services. According to the principles of comparative advantage, a region ought to be noncompetitive in goods it ought to import—just as it will be competitive in the goods it will succeed in exporting.

A crude view would be this: Half a nation's goods it competitively exports; half it will import, because domestic resources and know-how are not favorable or advantageous for producing those items in comparison with technology and endowments abroad. Half and half makes for balance, with no trade surplus or trade deficit.

Act I: Keeping the Balance in Balance

Since everything is always in flux, what keeps the balance in balance? Equilibrium is supposed to be maintained by the market mechanism. If certain lands and skills can't find market demand for their services, their price gets bid down in the auction market. At the right price they get the work they seek. This process of flexible clearing of the market is expedited internationally by automatic depreciation of the floating dollar relative to the appreciating Japanese yen when technological progress abroad is catching up in sectors where previously Yankee ingenuity was triumphant. When the dollar price of the yen becomes right, the trade balance will re-attain balance.

Three cheers for the floating exchange-rate system. In 1925 Britain foolishly returned to the gold standard at the 1913 prewar parity. She was foolish because in the intervening dozen years her price level and wage rates had risen more than had America's. Beginning anew with an overvalued British pound, very many U.K. industries were no longer cost competitive in the years leading up to the Great Depression. Chronic unemployment prevailed. Whatever the merits of the orthodox economist's prescription that by lowering wage rates full employment could be restored in the U.K., de facto costs tended to be sticky.

Notice that thus far my account has said nothing about improving management to achieve competitiveness. It has said naught about tariffs, quotas, and unlevel playing fields. It has taken no notice of the fact that U.S. society now has curtailed its rate of saving, absolutely and relative to saving rates abroad. It has gratuitously pretended that capital movements are supposed to net out to zero in international equilibrium rather than systematically adjusting themselves to differential rates of regional thriftiness.

Has my profundity been at the expense of your unease? Does deep analysis tell us at the end of the day that the chronic bilateral payments deficit between the U.S. and Japan is no sign of pathology at all but rather is completely in accordance with economic law? If this were the complete verdict, then much of the diplomatic skirmishing that goes on between President Clinton and Mickey Kantor on the one hand, and the Japanese negotiators on the other hand, would be only the minuet of an elaborate charade. A bit like wrestling on TV, more a ballet than a genuine grudge fight. If only for microeconomic reasons, matters are not that clear-cut. There are important interferences with free trade between our two nations—more perhaps on the Japanese than on our side—which need to be addressed and reduced to our mutual advantages. Then bilateral deficits may irreducibly remain, but they will be intrinsic to the situation rather than signs of misbehavior by either society.

Act II: Why Japan Owes the World a Recovery Effort

Now I shift gears and turn from Act I to Act II. I need to elucidate how and why Japan's current mishandling of her recession acts to make her unfairly competitive and to undermine American competitiveness. This topic has nothing to do with whether Japan's management style is or was effective, or with whether American schoolkids spend too much time with their faces mesmerized before a TV screen and too little time with their noses in a mathematical calculus book.

Japan's slump is self-prolonged. It is essentially due to a C performance by the Bank of Japan, a D performance by the Ministry of Finance, an E performance by the Cabinet, Diet, and new Prime Minister, and an F grade record earned by the Japanese electorate itself. Of course I am talking as an economics professor and not a philosopher. For all I know every member of the Diet is a kind and thoughtful family person, with a fine aesthetic interest in the arts of paper folding.

Japan has copious international reserves to provide needed elbowroom. Japan's public debt compared to GDP is the least constraining of any major power. Inflation in Japan is no problem at all, now or after remedial activisms. By not effectuating domestic stimulus, Japan is relying on export-led stimulus. Thereby she penalizes the American locomotive for being the first to help drag the world out of the current recession.

This is not right. Let me illustrate by something I learned from Professor Sato, which has confirmed what I had expected on a priori grounds as being about to happen.

Honda builds cars in America; builds them maybe more cheaply here than there, now that the dollar has fallen and the yen has appreciated. But Honda in Japan is pledged to give steady employment without layoffs. She pays her workers even if there is no profitable work for them to do. Since the true marginal costs of producing at home are zero, even though full fixed costs are colossal, it is smart for Honda to lay off the cheap American workers and bring the jobs back home. The longtime "hollowing out of Japan" begins to go into reverse as a second-best adaptation to the recession. "Smart" you say? "An act of economic aggression," I say. This is the kind of thing that invites Japan-bashing and bad feeling.

In any case, it is all so avoidable. If internal Japanese stimulus restores genuine high employment in Japan, not only will the long-neglected infrastructure be improved, but in addition equality will be restored for Japanese corporations between the wage they pay domestic workers and the sellable product produced by them. The "hollowing out" process will be resumed, to Japan's long-term advantage, precisely as in the case of other nations.

Act III: High Technology à la Schumpeter

Again, I shift gears abruptly and conclude with some observations about high technology. Consider a leading Fortune 500 American corporation back in the days when ours was pretty much a closed economy. Dupont will do as an example of a chemical giant, or GE as a high-tech producer of innovative electrical products.

These big boys pay high wages. They provide expensive fringe benefits for their workers. They have to, in order to successfully keep out the unions. Being highly profitable and committed to the high overhead of an elaborate structure of plant and equipment, they would be very vulnerable to any lasting strike or work stoppage.

"Life for them," my old Harvard teacher Josef Schumpeter would say, "is dangerous. They are anything but Absolute Monarchs. Like Queen Victoria and unlike Henry VIII, a constitutional monarch 'reigns as long as he doesn't rule.' The vicious, competitive marketplace asks of everybody: 'What have you done for me recently?' " (As an aside, let me say that the Schumpeter I first knew back in 1935 at Harvard did not seem to believe that these temporary celebrities—call them Andy Warhols, if you wish—would have permanent lasting power. For Schumpeter, capitalism is a hotel. Its luxury suites are always occupied, but ever by different tenants. The King is dead! Long live the King! During the last 15 years of Schumpeter's life I believe he changed his mind about dynamic oligopolies, becoming more persuaded that by scientific method they could learn the magic of perpetual youth. I'm not sure which Schumpeter was right.)

Back to work after the digression. In any case, uneasy rests the head of the high-tech leader. You may develop a great new electric light bulb. Fine for you. Produce it exquisitely in your high-rent factories. Charge a high markup, knowing that your product is in temporary monopoly scarcity.

But the story does not end there. If no new innovations continue to occur, soon effective knowledge will spread and a nonunion shop will be able to run off assembly-line electric bulbs almost as good as yours and leave your market high and dry. Yes, Dupont can produce and sell standard sulfuric acid at low-margin prices. But never can it stay at the top of the Fortune 500 by the likes of that. A new Nylon must be followed by a new Orlon or Duco car paint if it is to hold its market share. That is the fate of the lead bicycle racer. It is he who must break the wind for the eager followers. They can coast on his airflow. No coasting for him.

Remember this when your tally shows that Boeing still has comparative advantage in aircraft production, even though all of Eastman's cameras are now being produced in Indonesia or Tijuana. Tomorrow Nagoya will be the hot spot for jet airfoil design if somewhere in America there cannot be found resources to plow the frontier of scientific research and managerial-engineering practice.

The cold war was a terrible thing. But one of its spin-offs was the B-52 bomber, which provided something of a free ride for the development of the 407 and its progeny of commercial jet models. Predictability about the new and unknown is irreducibly hazardous. The trends of high productivity will therefore always be more uncertain than those of routine mass productions.

If time were not so scarce I could hope to speculate about why Japan may have a special motive to subsidize high-tech research, even beyond finding new laws of science and technology. Maybe its oligopolistic structure motivates spending a million and a half yen in order to harvest a million yen worth of useful knowledge? If so, the Japanese consuming public will not be the primary beneficiaries.

PART TWO

Lectures from Spring 1994

CHAPTER 4

Recent Developments in International Financial Markets: Implications to Japan and the United States

February 15, 1994

INTRODUCTORY REMARKS

ROBERT KAVESH: We have a timely program. Today's *New York Times* carries the headline: "U.S. Taking Action against Japanese in One Trade Case." Then, underneath the fold, an economics article by Peter Passell: "Big Trade Deficit with Japan: Some Think It's No Problem." But just a few days ago we saw President Clinton and Prime Minister Hosokawa of Japan standing next to each other, almost defiantly—maybe that's too strong a term—saying, "This shall not pass or stand." So we are embroiled in controversies, but controversies are the warp and woof of what really goes on. Today's theme is "Recent Developments in International Financial Markets: Implications to Japan and the United States."

Our three panelists will speak fairly briefly on topics that are related but not exactly synchronized. Let me set the stage, because this is important material. It is filled with rhetoric, and oftentimes behind the rhetoric there really isn't that much in the way of substance. But people have roles to play, and these roles frequently are much more than simple economic roles. And that gets us into the topic.

We have Stephen Figlewski, Professor of Finance at the Stern School and a widely published scholar. He is the editor of the *Journal of Derivatives*. And Steve, pray for derivatives. But we'll hear more about that perhaps later on. Also widely published is our second speaker, Yasushi Hamao, a Professor at Columbia University. He was educated at Tokyo University and at Yale. Third is Professor Paul A. Samuelson, in my opinion and in the opinion of many people in this field of economics, the Economist for the Twentieth Century.

STEPHEN FIGLEWSKI

I'd like to thank the Japan-U.S. Center and Professor Sato for inviting me to speak to you this morning. The topic, "Recent Developments in International Financial Markets," lends itself to the kind of presentation that I don't often make. When people come to public discussions like this, typically what they really want to know are things like: "Which way are financial markets going to go?" "Where are the best profit opportunities going to turn up in the near future?" So in thinking about what I was going to say to you this morning, I decided to try and give you my predictions on these matters.

I quickly realized how hard it is to make justifiable forecasts of such things. In attempting to come up with a set of intelligent predictions for this talk I discovered once again how many important things there are that I don't really feel I have any special information about that's not widely available to everybody.

Where are short-term interest rates going to go? In the last two weeks we've seen a major move by the Federal Reserve. It was actually a small move in terms of percentage change. They increased the target rate for the Federal funds rate by a quarter of a percent, but it had quite an impact on the market. The question at this point is, what's going to happen next? Are we going to go along for a while with no further increase in interest rates? Or is this just the first step in a long, sharp rise in interest rates, back perhaps to the levels of the 1980s? Where are short interest rates going to go?

Where are long-term interest rates going to go? In the last year and a half, the yield on the long-term Treasury bond in the U.S. dropped from about $7\frac{1}{2}$ percent to under 6 percent and then bounced back up to where it is right now, around 6.4 percent. Is this a good time or a bad time to be buying bonds? Which way is the bond market going to go?

Which way is the stock market going to go? 1993 was a pretty good year for stocks. As the long bonds were going up in value, so was the stock market and this has continued in this year. We are flirting with a DOW of 4,000. It may well happen in the next few weeks. Or are we at the peak, heading down toward lower levels in the stock market?

What investment strategies are going to turn out to be hot this year? Should we be buying small stocks? Should we be buying cyclical stocks? Especially in view of recent developments in Washington, what is the Japan-U.S. trade balance going to do? A key part of the whole puzzle, what's the exchange rate on the yen going to do? Finally, what's the Japanese stock market going to do?

These are all questions that everybody would love to know the answers to, and I wish I could give you forecasts that would contain a whole lot of information that wouldn't be widely available to other people. But of course if I could do that I'd probably be out managing portfolios of billions of dollars rather than teaching.

So what can I say about these topics that everybody wants to know the answer to? Since what I do is teach, I began to think about what I would tell an MBA class about these questions. I decided to start with some of the fundamental principles that we teach to MBAs, and see how we can apply these ideas to the questions that I just raised.

One of the most important things that I try to get across in the classroom is that freely operating financial markets are informationally efficient, or at least very close to it, which implies that the price you see in the market contains a great deal of information. It's the result of a whole lot of intelligent people all trying to trade and take advantage of information that they may have, so that the market ends up pricing securities based on the combined information of a lot of intelligent people.

What would we say to an MBA class about some of the specific questions that I raised? Well, short-term nominal interest rates are set by the Federal Reserve. Where are short-term rates going to go this year? Inherently, we have to forecast what the Federal Reserve is going to do. Long-term interest rates are largely determined by expectations about what the short-term rate is going to do. So we can look at combining these three first ideas: We can look at long-term interest rates in the market and get some idea about what the market is predicting short-term interest rates are going to be doing in the near future.

What about the stock market? One strong principle we believe is that the equilibrium rate of return on a risky asset like stock should be equal to the riskless rate of interest plus some appropriate risk premium. We will use that principle to say something about what the market thinks the stock market is going to do. Another big principle that crops up time and again is that diversification as an investment strategy pays off. It's a way of reducing risk without necessarily reducing return. Finally, to say something about the trade balance, a basic principle is that the balance of payments is an accounting identity. The balance of payments must balance.

Let's see how those things can lead us to some answers to the questions that I raised. First, what about short-term interest rates? By the expectations theory of the term structure of interest, today's interest rate for a two-year instrument impounds today's rate for a one-year instrument and what the market thinks one-year instruments will be yielding a year from now. So the compounded return over two years for buying a two-year instrument should be one plus the rate you get in the first year times one plus the rate the market expects you'll be able to get a year from now.

Right now if you look in the newspaper at one-year Treasury zero coupon bonds or Treasury strips, a one-year instrument is yielding 3.96 percent and a two-year instrument is yielding 4.51 percent. We can solve and figure out what the market must expect the one-year rate to be a year from now from the pricing of two-year instruments at 4.51 percent. The answer, according to this theory anyway, is the market thinks that the short-term interest rate (the one-year rate) a year from now is going to be a little bit above 5 percent.

What can we say about long bonds? The expectations theory of the term structure also says that all fixed income instruments should be priced so that they yield the same amount or are expected to yield the same amount over a given period of time. So the long bond is priced now so that it is expected to earn the one-year rate over the next year. Well, the one-year rate is 3.96 percent, as we just saw. Let's see what that means for what's going to happen to the 30 year Treasury. The 30 year Treasury, the "on-the-run" Treasury right now, is the $6\frac{1}{4}$ percent coupon of August 2023, which was priced in the market last Friday at $97\frac{28}{32}$ with a yield to maturity of 6.41 percent. Owning this bond, over this next year you're going to get $6.26 per $100 face value in coupon interest. So the coupon yield is over 6 percent. Total yield though, in order to match the one-year short rate, has to be only 3.96 percent.

That means the market must be forecasting that this bond is going to go down in price, so the yield to maturity on it is going to go up. We can solve through this and figure out that, in order for this bond to have a total yield of 3.96 percent over the year, the market is forecasting the price is going to go down to 95.44, a little bit under $95\frac{1}{2}$. At that price a year from now that bond will have a yield to maturity of 6.61 percent. So inherent in today's term structure is the forecast that the long rate is going to go up 20 basis points over the year.

How about stocks? The equilibrium rate of return on risky assets like stock should be equal to the riskless rate plus an appropriate risk premium. Since 1948, the mean rate of return on the S&P 500 including dividends has been 12.7 percent, while the mean three-month Treasury bill yield has been 5.6 percent. That means the risk premium for the last 46 years is 7.1 percent on stocks. Let's take today's short-term rate, the $3\frac{1}{4}$ percent we see in the market on a three-month bill, add that 7.1 percent premium, and we get a fair return on stocks of 10.35 percent. Some of that is expected to come in the form of dividends, and the rest in the form of capital gains. Right now the dividend yield on the S&P 500 is about 2.7 percent, so that means this 10.35 percent total return should come from 2.7 percent dividend yield and about 7.65 percent price appreciation. Right now the S&P Index is about 470. With a 7.65 percent increase, we get the forecast inherent in today's market of 506.

Now before you think this is pretty precise, I should also say that the standard deviation around that 10.35 percent is about 14 percent a year. So if I were to put a one standard deviation confidence range around where the S&P 500 is going to be a year from now, you'd get a range from 436 to 568. If we want 95 percent confidence we'd better have two standard deviations. I will say with a high degree of confidence that the S&P 500 a year from now will be somewhere between 370 and 633. Unfortunately, it's hard to make really strong investment decisions on the basis of that forecast.

How about the hot investment strategies? Actually I'm more confident in this than I am in some of the other things I've said. The basic principle at work here is that diversification pays. Americans are investing very heavily in mutual funds. They're letting institutions invest for them rather than playing the market themselves. Net inflows in 1993 were $128 billion to mutual funds, and that's more than the total in 1991 and 1992 combined. Total holdings in mutual funds are over $2 trillion.

We also see diversification internationally. American investors have in the past been very provincial. American portfolios have no more than about 5 percent invested in foreign equities. This is very small. In the classroom, we say the appropriate investment strategy is to hold the market portfolio. In an internationally integrated financial market the market portfolio that is relevant is the whole world market portfolio, and Americans are a long way from being invested in that. But we're changing. In the first three quarters of 1993, over $40 billion were invested in purchases of foreign equities by U.S. funds. And by the end of 1993 a total over $110 billion was invested in mutual funds that specialize in buying international equities.

Now we come to one of the hard questions, because I don't consider myself an expert on the Japanese economy at all. But there are some principles here about the fact that the balance of payments is an accounting identity that should affect the way we think about what's going on right now concerning the trade questions that are on the table.

Since a balance of payments must balance as a matter of accounting, an imbalance in the capital account must be offset by an opposite imbalance in the trade balance. In other words, if we are going to import more than we export, then we have to find people who are going to lend us the money to do that. So a balance of trade deficit will be offset in our overall balance of payments by a surplus in the capital account—more money flowing in for investment purposes than is flowing out.

As long as the United States as a nation spends more than it produces and finances this shortfall by borrowing money from foreigners, we will be running a surplus on the capital account, more money coming in than we are lending overseas, and this will mirror a deficit on the current account. Therefore, we are bound to run a trade deficit as long as we are borrowing more from foreigners than we are lending to them.

The mirror image of this is Japan. In Japan the nation consumes less than it produces, and it lends money to other countries. Japan produces goods and doesn't consume them all. The remainder goes for exports. These are financed by capital flows from Japan to the rest of the world, and as long as this continues, as long as the Japanese are more thrifty than Americans are as a nation, they will run a surplus on current account.

All the trade issues that we're making so much noise about right now reveal how this imbalance, caused by the different savings and spending behavior in the two countries, is going to be worked out. Things like opening the Japanese markets to U.S. products, while they may affect what goods are traded, are not going to change the overall current account deficit until we end up in more balance as far as our consumption and production are concerned. As we go forward, the reduction in the U.S. federal budget deficit in future years and the increase in output as our economy picks up should moderate our balance of payments problems, but it won't do away with them all.

What are the Japanese stock market and the exchange rate on the yen going to do? I really have a hard time giving you a good answer to this one. Freely operating financial markets are informationally efficient, but these are two areas where there's reason to doubt if the markets are in fact going to be freely operating. Government intervention can push prices away from where an efficient market would put them. Intervention can work in the short run although it tends to be extremely costly and doesn't generally work in the long run.

Governments are nevertheless especially prone to attempt to manipulate exchange rates. We also have seen that some Japanese government policy seems to be directed toward the stock market as well. What's going to happen in those markets will depend, I think, a great deal on how the two countries behave in attempting to either prop up the stock market or to affect the exchange rate one way or another.

Another trend we've seen in the last couple of years is more and more activity by what are called hedge funds. These are investment portfolios run by people who are looking for low-risk, high-return strategies to capitalize on disequilibrium pricing in the market. George Soros makes a lot of money by betting against foreign governments who are trying to prop up their exchange rate when they can't do that over the long run, and we're seeing more and more of that in the market.

Although I started out saying that I don't think I have any special information, I would like to suggest that just as we have found over the years that it is extremely hard for an active stock picker to beat the stock market, I think it's awfully hard for an active economic forecaster to beat the kind of predictions inherent in the type of analysis I have just given you, basing those predictions on the assumption that the financial markets are efficient.

YASUSHI HAMAO

I would like to thank Professor Sato and the Center for Japan-U.S. Business and Economic Studies for having me today. I will be talking about the Japanese stock market, in comparison with the U.S. market.

When you look at newspapers to see how the Nikkei stock average is doing, you will notice that the volatility is quite high; it is not unusual to have two or more percentage points up or down in one day. Recently this seems to be driven mostly by government announcements on policy changes, for example, how political reform is going to be done, whether there will be an income tax cut, or how the U.S.-Japan trade negotiation is coming along.

These are undoubtedly important issues that would shape up the Japanese stock market, but are these all that matter? At the micro level, stock prices should also reflect the fundamentals of firms, that is, how the firms are doing in their business. I am going to present some evidence that Japanese investors have paid little attention to this matter. Instead, the market seems to have been overwhelmed by general euphoria during the bubble period (before 1990) and by general pessimism after the burst of the bubble.

This research, conducted by Charles Hall, Trevor Harris (two colleagues of mine at Columbia), and myself, looks at the relations between earnings of firms and their stock prices over a long time horizon. (These findings are published as "A Comparison of Relation between Security Market Prices, Returns and Accounting Measures in Japan and the United States" in the *Journal of International Financial Management and Accounting*, Vol. 5–5, 1994.) If investors are rational, there should be a positive relation. Of course the reported accounting earnings contain errors and possible manipulation. In a one-year horizon the relation between earnings and stock price would be weak, but by expanding the time horizon to say ten or twenty years, these measurement errors tend to be canceled out and you would have a more significant association.

Formally, we regress cross-sectionally stock returns over the observation period on accumulated earnings and the change in earnings over the same period of time. We choose the observation period ("window" of measurement) to be one year, four years, seven years, and twenty years. We look at R_2 (correlation) from these cross-section regressions. This measures how much variation in stock returns is explained by earnings. The higher the R^2, the more association between stock prices and earnings.

In a one-year window, the R_2 is very low for both Japan and the U.S. In Japan it is mostly less than 10 percent. In the U.S. the numbers are not as low as in Japan, but still you find much "noise." We also notice that in Japan the association was particularly weak during the 1980s, when the "bubble" was forming. When we expand the window to four years and seven years, the R_2 gets higher in both countries. In the U.S. it gets as high as 50 percent, while in Japan it is still lower than in the U.S.—around 10 percent.

A very interesting observation is that if we look at those windows ending in 1990 and 1991, we find much higher association in Japan. This is true for one year, but even more dramatic in longer windows. The bubble in the Japanese stock market burst at the beginning of 1990. Our data run only two years after that, but already we appear to capture a change in the relation between the stock price and company fundamentals. You may say that there was an "anything goes" kind of attitude during the bubble period, when stock prices were running up irrespective of earnings and other fundamentals. But the trend seems to be reverting after 1990. Back to fundamentals: After the collapse of the bubble, the investors may be paying more attention to how the company itself is doing.

PAUL A. SAMUELSON

On the morning after a California earthquake measuring 6.6 on the Richter scale, a lecturer on the tranquility of nature finds it optimal to revise her text in some perceptible degree. This morning's scheduled discussion of Japan-U.S. financial developments can hardly fail to take notice of last weekend's impasse between Prime Minister Morihiro Hosokawa and President William Clinton.

This morning's newspapers—the *New York Times,* the *Washington Post,* and the *Wall Street Journal* (do any others matter?)—are full of this subject. Let me say that speaking as an academic economist, an American patriot, and a well-wisher to Japan, in none of these roles do I regard the failure of the two leaders to reach any meeting of the minds as an event registering 6.0 on the political economy Richter scale. Still, who am I against the world? Yesterday the dollar fell from 108 yen to 102, truly a "big one" for highly leveraged traders in the futures markets. The aftershocks still sure to come may outweigh the Washington event itself.

As they say, there is good news and bad news. That's what one of my daughters-in-law said to me recently. "Which do you want to hear first?" "Give me the good news," I said. "Well, today Cooper said 'Mama.' That's the good news. The bad news is that he said it to the babysitter." The good news is that the Japanese people are understandably tired of being harangued by Americans. They are tired of having to babble meaningless phrases of agreement to do things that nobody has any expectations will get done. So for the moment Hosokawa gains in popularity at home for standing tall and telling off the American President as a mature equal.

This is a time, I suspect, when a boost to the Japanese ego and morale is especially needed. The collapse of the land and stock-market booms and the ensuing serious recession have engendered something of a failure of Japanese nerve—a veritable self-identity crisis based on serious doubts about the validity of the Japanese economic model.

An inveterate optimist could go on to argue:

The new Prime Minister has been popular in the polls, but it has not been a popularity you could cash out at the bank in effective political action. In effect his coalition has been one made of tissue paper—a coalition unable to put through the drastic macroeconomic policies that are desperately needed to stem the serious slump. In consequence, Japan has been essentially a ship at sea without a rudder and with sails chaotically aligned so as to catch no winds in motion.

An inveterate optimist, determined to find a silver lining in every dark cloud, could go on to argue in the following vein:

The Washington deadlock was in fact a fortuitous turn in the political tide. It will give Japan's leader the extra popularity and leverage to move finally in the decisive way that is badly needed. When next the G-7 meet, Japan will have contrived a truly expansionary fiscal program, and her crash program of monetary ease will have launched her GDP recovery at a 4 percent per annum rate.

Blessed be Machiavelli, whose Invisible Hand is seen once again to triumph! If you can believe in this rosy scenario, you have credentials to be a voting member in the Academy of the Tooth Fairy.

What is the bad-news version of the future? It goes like this:

1. The Mid-February disagreements in Washington are only an early move in an ongoing chess game. The ball is now in the Japanese court. If an anti-climax of no further action ensues, then an American reaction must be expected.

2. Bill Clinton is already under criticism for failing to follow through on his tough talk. Innocent humans are killed in Yugoslavia. Clinton warns that this is intolerable and that American might will punish the wrongdoers, but the prospects for the American people of another Vietnam quagmire lead to a Clinton backdown. Smarting under criticism of his irresolution, Clinton and his hawkish trade negotiators can curry popularity at home by getting tough with trade sanctions. If American producers don't achieve X percent of the Japanese semiconductor market by the Fourth of July, all imports from Japan in the electronics category will be levied an import surcharge of Y percent and a quota reduction of

Z percent. If Fidelity, Dreyfus, and Vanguard are not permitted to gain 35 percent of the pension-management business in Japan by April Fool's Day, then notebook computers made in Japan are declared contraband in Iowa. You can outline similar ultimatums that go into effect by Flag Day, June 14 or Bastille Day, July 14.

Of course you listeners will understand that my tongue is in my cheek. I am not seriously predicting either a soft landing in which every prospect pleases or the beginning of a Thirty Years' War that will lead to the end of civilization as we have known it. I write in the spirit of George Bernard Shaw, who said: "Never strike a child except in anger." I never make a joke unless it serves to advance a serious point.

I am 100 percent serious in saying:

Expect Clinton, his trade representative Mickey Kantor, and Deputy Secretary of Treasury Robert Altman to react in some punitive way against Japan if she makes no new conciliatory move. Saving of face will demand it. Moreover, actions taken under such motivations are especially prone to be unwise—non-optimal from the standpoint of both parties' self-interest.

Mind you, most of us economists are unsympathetic to the Kantor-Altman gambit of demanding that Japan agree to meet specific numerical targets of physical imports or percentage shares of markets by agreed-upon dates. That does not mean we economists approve of the myriad formal and informal mechanisms that Japan employs to protect domestic interests. Nor does it mean that we doubt that threats can sometimes succeed in moving political mountains that are harmful to everybody.

Rather, it is a truth that threats come to lack credibility if never they are used. If the nature of the threats themselves is to create bilateral deadweight losses, then a mode of negotiating that relies on such threats is liable to turn Positive-Sum trade scenarios into Zero-Sum or Negative-Sum scenarios.

Let me wind up by outlining briefly what Japan ought to be doing now in her own interest and as an important player in the global economy and the community of nations. What can good friends of Japan legitimately urge upon her?

First, we should separate two problems:

1. the GDP problem of current production, employment, and income;
2. the balance-sheet problem of the solvency of the banks and the need to restore their capital in relation to their investments and liabilities.

The two problems are, of course, related. For example, when banks are desperately short of capital they will not extend loans to potential employers of workers.

The new coalition government has fallen behind on both fronts. On the first problem of recessionary GDP it should do three things:

1. The Bank of Japan should be persuaded or coerced into massively expanding credit. This will mean interest rates definitely below the inflation rate. Negative real interest rates are the prudent target until the recession is clearly defeated. It is bad scientific economics that monetary policy has already shot its bolt.

2. Income tax rates should be cut across the board. At this time no promises should be made about raising them again in the future or offsetting them with future new indirect taxes. Silence is golden.

3. Cyclical expansion in deficit-financed fiscal expenditures should be the order of the day. Only after activist macro programs have brought back sustained recovery should government turn back toward more austere fiscal policies.

What about the banks? The Japanese voters may think that the government ought not to bail out the banks from the mistakes that they themselves made. But it will be the Japanese people who will be most hurt if the government allows a replay in Japan of the Herbert Hoover scenario of 1929–33, in which thousands of American banks on Main Street were allowed to fail and close their doors forever.

Every society needs a viable banking system. By hypocrisy or otherwise, the Diet and the bureaucracy must set up a Rescue Corporation to replenish the gone-forever assets of the banks. Send your experts to Washington to study how President Bush and President Clinton have dealt, dealt successfully, with America's banking crisis.

We in America have turned the corner. By 1995 Japan can do so, too. But not if she continues her 1990–94 macro-pattern of drift and passivism.

CHAPTER 5

Financial Developments in Europe, Japan, and the United States: Problems and Prospects

April 11, 1994

INTRODUCTORY REMARKS

ROBERT KAVESH: Professor Willem Buiter comes to us from Yale University, where he has had a distinguished career. It is interesting that he's the Juan Trippe Professor of International Economics, because those of you who go back some years will remember that Juan Trippe was one of the founders of Pan American Airlines. In a discussion of international economics and finance it's interesting to ask, "What ever happened to Pan American?" What ever happened to a lot of companies?

Professor Richard Levich has been on the faculty at the Stern School for several years. He's a University of Chicago graduate through and through, which means he is a man of strong opinions, which he will share with us a little bit later on. Toru Kusukawa is Chairman of the Fuji Research Institute Corporation, and before the meeting started today he and I were talking about the fact that some day all the fighting might be over and people of goodwill around the world could do serious things like gardening. That may happen some day. Of course Professor Samuelson, who has been here for several years and on many, many occasions, is quite simply the Greatest Economist of the Twentieth Century.

WILLEM H. BUITER

Regarding Professor Kavesh's introduction, I hope my intellectual health is better than the financial health of Pan Am, which has been defunct for some time. I will focus on some very broad-ranging issues, including the international monetary and exchange rate regime, international trade imbalances, and the importance of not confusing them with competitiveness problems.

For the international monetary and exchange rate regime, I think there is now virtually universal consensus. For the foreseeable future there is no alternative to a dirty float. A float, because any attempt to fix key exchange rates is inconsistent with the degree of national sovereignty remaining among the major industrial countries in the presence of the kind of capital mobility that we've known, that we've grown to know and love. It has to be a dirty float, not a clean float, because governments never can leave anything alone and therefore the whole notion of a clean float is a construct that has never found any applicability.

This holds with the Big Three—the D-mark, the dollar and the yen—and also importantly within the European Union. The exchange rate mechanism is dead, at least for this century. I do believe that there will be a European Monetary Union, a West European Monetary Union we should call it really, but I do not expect it until some time in the next decade, the beginning of the twenty-first century rather than the end of the twentieth century. The reasons for that are too many to go into, but basically and fundamentally a greater degree of political sovereignty will have to be transferred to the central European administration if the fixed exchange rate regime central to the European Monetary Union is going to be credible. We learned this in a lot of painful ways, in a way that has exacerbated the European recession, but we've learned it now so let's not try and resurrect horses that should remain dead.

I am in the unusual position of not finding much to criticize in the United States. For once I think both monetarily and fiscally the U.S. authorities have got it right. This I don't think has ever happened before, except perhaps when Paul Samuelson was advising the U.S. government.

For a number of years, in fact until recently, the Fed pursued a resolutely expansive monetary policy, like its silly sisters in Europe and to a certain extent in Japan. The Fed also decided, wisely, very recently, that the danger was if anything in overheating, and some moderate monetary stance was required. The fact that the market panicked at the sight of a quarter of a percent increase in short-term interest rates is more a reflection on the markets and their almost unlimited capacity at least for short-term frivolity than on monetary policies.

Fiscally the Clinton administration is moving ahead with measures which, given the kind of growth we're seeing now, should make the U.S. budget position sustainable. The same cannot be said of Europe or Japan. Both Europe and Japan need stimuli. Europe, still to a large extent in thrall to the Bundesbank, is stuck with interest rates which are well above what is desirable, and this could be remedied with or without the Bundesbank if people were willing to forgo the largely illusionary benefits, especially in the case of France, of shadowing the still overly strong D-mark. Europe needs financial relaxation, and Japan needs a mixture of financial and fiscal relaxation. Very little is actually happening there, disappointingly, and I think criticism can be rightly leveled at Japanese macroeconomic policy, including monetary policy, not primarily for trade balance reasons, but simply because it is not a policy that makes sense even from an internal Japanese perspective of utilization and demand.

Regarding my last point, the quickest way of making it is to say that international trade relations are in a good news/bad news phase, and part of the bad news is due to the tendency, most emphatically present in the Clinton administration, to confuse macroeconomic imbalances with competitiveness problems. The good news in international trade relations is the completion in all but the signing of the Uruguay Round and the conclusion of NAFTA. It is to the credit of the Clinton administration that they managed to pull these off. The bad news is that there is a hardening if anything in the more industrial countries of protectionist instincts. This I've learned is more true in the U.S. than even in Europe or Japan. I'm talking trends, not levels. The level of protectionism is highest in Japan, but

132

the strongest pressure for increasing the level of protectionism is undoubtedly in the United States, which is going through a singularly bad phase.

It is important to recognize that the trade surpluses of Japan, both its overall trade surplus and its bilateral trade surplus with the United States, are macroeconomic phenomena, not the reflection of competitiveness problems and not the reflection of protectionist tendencies in either country. It will be cured by macroeconomic developments, not by changes in competitiveness, nor by changes in protectionism. The Japanese could introduce unrestricted market access for all comers tomorrow without in any obvious way changing the overall trade balance.

The trade balance, as macroeconomists never tire of pointing out, is the excess of national saving over domestic capital formation. While the Japanese invest impressively compared to most of the other industrial countries, they save even more impressively. Instead of criticizing them for that, the rest of world should go down on its knees and be thankful that at least somebody is providing the world with the capital that is needed. I just read this morning in the *Financial Times* that Latin America imported capital equal to 3.8 percent of its GDP last year. It has to come from somewhere. It's not going to come from here, right? The United States and most of Europe have lost the saving habit altogether. Japan still saves. It is true that the present high Japanese saving rate is partly cyclical, and I would therefore support further fiscal and monetary measures to increase Japanese domestic spending.

I would hope that the recovery of Japanese domestic demand will not be accompanied by a disappearance of the financial surpluses. The former Soviet Union, Southeast Asia, South America, Central America, and Northern Africa all need large injections of investable funds. These sorts of surpluses are being generated only in Japan and that is the place where we should hope they remain, unless we really believe that the United States is ready as a nation to up the national saving rate by 4 or 5 or maybe 10 percent of the GDP to take over the role the Japanese are being asked to give up. Surely not. This will not happen. By all means take measures, hopefully at a multilateral level, to reduce the protectionist habits ingrained in the Japanese economy. But don't attack the Japanese for the one success in their external economic policies, their trade surpluses.

RICHARD LEVICH

Professor Sato has given the panel today a large canvas—Financial Developments in Europe, Japan, and the United States: Problems and Prospects—perhaps so that each speaker will not feel constrained and may paint over as large or small a portion of the canvas as he chooses. While I might normally be expected to discuss foreign exchange markets, their efficiency or forecasting, my theme today will be the challenge for setting policy in the financial derivatives market.

By derivatives I mean the collection of futures, forwards, options, and swaps—securities that derive their value from underlying assets such as foreign exchange, bonds, short-term interest-rate obligations, equities, and other assets of value. Derivative securities may exist on their own or may be imbedded within other securities. Derivative securities may be traded on centralized exchanges—as commodity futures have been for many years, as foreign exchange futures have since the early 1970s, or as interest rate futures have since the early 1980s. Centralized exchanges within the United States and elsewhere are regulated, providing a measure of investor protection and safeguards (such as procedures for margin requirements, clearing, and settlement) against risks in one market spilling over into other parts of the financial system.

The growth of financial futures and options contracts has been spectacular. In 1993 more than one billion exchange-traded futures and options contracts traded hands on 62 exchanges around the world.[1] The top contract in 1993 was the U.S. Treasury Bond futures traded on the Chicago Board of Trade (CBOT) with an average daily volume of over 300,000 contracts.[2] Each contract represents $100,000 in underlying government securities, making an average day represent over $30 billion in notional value. The second most actively traded contract, the Eurodollar futures contract on the Chicago Mercantile Exchange (CME), had a daily trading volume of only 250,000 contracts.[3] But with each Eurodollar futures contract representing $1 million, an average day's trading of this single contract represents $250 billion in notional value.

While these numbers are large even to congressmen and professional athletes, they are modest in comparison to the over-the-counter (OTC) market for financial derivatives. A recent government (joint FRB/FDIC/OCC) study estimated the notional size of banks' exposure in OTC derivatives (including forwards, options, and swaps) at $8 trillion in 1992.[4] Further, the study found that 90 percent of the exposure among banks was concentrated in only seven bank holding companies—making the argument for quality risk management in these institutions essential, but also suggesting the ease with which this highly concentrated banking and financial activity could be regulated.

This is where the story for today's topic really begins.

Shortly after Professor Sato asked me to participate in this panel, I heard a speech by Representative Jim Leach of Iowa, the senior Republican on the House Banking Panel. Representative Leach has issued a 900-page study on the OTC derivatives market that recommends an interagency commission to establish uniform capital rules, accounting, disclosure, and suitability standards for dealers and end-users of derivatives. The study underpins legislation calling for the creation of a new Federal Derivatives Commission (FDC). Representative Henry Gonzalez, the Chairman of the House Banking Committee, is putting forward his own legislation on derivatives.[5]

Now the federal government, along with regulators in other countries, have a clear right to be concerned about the risk of a system-wide disturbance arising from the derivatives markets, especially the OTC market. Underlying their concern is the possibility that the official safety net has provided an implicit guarantee of banks' obligations, which in turn has unintentionally subsidized the OTC market. Perhaps this implicit guarantee has played a role in the rapid expansion of the derivatives markets, which has exposed the financial system to greater risk. Regulators are also concerned about the quality of senior management and the risk management systems that have been put into place. Regulators doubt their own and managers' ability to understand and manage these new complex transactions. Other factors, namely that derivatives help to strengthen the linkages across markets and increase the likelihood of spillovers, that these markets appear concentrated, and that systemic risks may be underpriced, emphasize the need for oversight.

We grant that there are reasons to be concerned about the growth of these new financial market products. But is the cry, "I'm from the federal government, and I'm here to help you" a welcome voice in this public policy debate? Past U.S. regulation of financial institutions has erred through both sins of commission and sins of omission, being at times too lenient and at times too strict. The international financial markets especially offer examples of the long-lasting and unintended consequences of U.S. regulation.

Example 1. The Eurocurrency markets, the offshore markets for short-term bank deposits and loans, grew up in the 1960s and 1970s in the shadow of a U.S. banking industry burdened with Regulation Q interest-rate ceilings and Regulation D non-interest-bearing reserve requirements. The Eurocurrency market today has grown to $7 trillion. In 1981, 20 years after the birth of the Eurocurrency market, the United States surrendered by allowing International Banking Facilities (IBFs) to handle offshore transactions within U.S. borders, but only for nonresidents. But with this late arrival, only 15 percent of offshore banking is captured by American-based IBFs.

Example 2. Along the same lines, the Eurobond market, the offshore market for long-term borrowing and lending, developed in the 1960s, and 1970s with the protective aid of U.S. regulations—the Interest Rate Equalization tax

(IET) and the Office of Foreign Direct Investment (OFDI) supervision. As one author notes: "Indeed, it is paradoxical that a law which was intentionally prejudicial to the interests of foreign borrowers [the IET] had the effect of creating the largest international capital market the world has known."[6] New-issue activity in the Eurobond market now regularly outstrips that in the U.S. market even though the IET and OFDI regulations were scrapped in 1974. The United States was even slower to respond to the Eurobond market, waiting until 1990 to introduce Rule 144a allowing securities (including foreign securities) to be issued to and traded among "qualified" institutional investors, with information disclosures determined by their own market practices rather than SEC guidelines.

Example 3. In equity markets, the U.S. has still not responded to world trends. The United States is the only marketplace that permits access on the basis of national treatment (i.e., requiring U.S. GAAP [generally accepted accounting principles] statements of all firms with exchange-traded equity shares), whereas other countries allow access to public markets on the basis of reciprocity (permitting home-country GAAP statements to suffice in most cases).

The prospect of fresh congressional legislation at this time is unsettling because so much progress has been made in addressing the shared concerns of regulators and market participants. Let me mention four examples.

1. Federal Reserve Regulation EE

The Federal Reserve recently issued Regulation EE, intended to strengthen the foundation for financial netting contracts that have been developed privately for use in foreign exchange, swaps, and other OTC products. In using these netting contracts, the counterparties agree that they will pay or receive net amounts due on a series of financial contracts or payment orders, rather than the gross amounts due on each obligation. To quote a Federal Reserve Governor: "The new regulation establishes relatively simple generic tests that will permit financial institutions, which are acting as market-makers, to enter into netting contracts that will be valid under federal law, even in the event of bankruptcy."[7] These netting contracts are extremely important, as they reduce the total net exposure to about 1 percent of the gross exposure amount.

2. Federal Reserve Fedwire Changes

Delivery risk—the chance that bankruptcy occurs between the payment of funds in one part of the world and the receipt of funds later in the day in another part of the world—is another important systemic risk. Lately, this has been termed "Herstatt risk" in recognition of the famous closure of the Herstatt Bank in 1974. This risk is especially acute in the case of yen-dollar contracts, where yen payments are often made and settled as much as 18 hours before dollar contra-payments are finally settled.

In February 1994 the Federal Reserve announced that beginning in 1997 the operating day for the Fedwire will be expanded from the current 10 hours to 18 hours. Specifically, the Fedwire funds transfer service will operate from 12:30 A.M. until 6:30 P.M. Eastern time. The change will essentially eliminate Herstatt risk between the U.S. and Europe, and potentially eliminate the risk between the U.S. and Japan.

3. Multilateral Clearing and Settlement

Private institutions have themselves been responsive to concerns expressed by ex-New York Federal Reserve Bank President Gerald Corrigan that daily trading volume in foreign exchange of more than $1 trillion poses a systemic risk from clearing and settlement. A new private company known as Multinet—a joint venture between International Clearing Systems Inc. (a subsidiary of Options Clearing Corporation) and North American Clearing House—has developed a system of multilateral netting in foreign exchange. To illustrate the power of multilateral clearing, imagine a world of 1,000 banks trading with each other. At the end of each day each bank would owe a net amount to each counterparty, resulting in as many as 500,000 bilateral transactions (in each currency of trade). In the multilateral system each bank clears with the central institution, resulting in no more than 1,000 transfers between each bank and the central agent. The amounts at risk to computer failures are greatly reduced by the privately-owned Multinet system. The system will be launched for foreign exchange trades in July 1995. Multinet is also planning to set up an OTC clearing house along the same lines.

4. Separately Capitalized "Derivative Guarantee" Corporations

Market-makers now clearly realize that counterparty risk is an invaluable asset for participating in the OTC derivatives markets. Major players in the market have set up separate, well-capitalized subsidiaries (the terminology is "bankruptcy remote"). The primary business objective of these subsidiaries is to obtain an S&P AAA rating to prove their creditworthiness, while at the same time holding a designated portion of the counterparty and market risks associated with its parent's derivatives portfolio. Reading the business plan of one of these guarantee firms is highly instructive about the nature of today's OTC derivatives business.[8] It is a clear signal of prudence on the part of management that they are willing to disclose their risk management systems to an independent rating agency (S&P) to obtain a credit rating that may be revoked or terminated if certain well-defined events occur. It is a clear indication that an "unregulated" market can actually be highly disciplined through self-regulation and the discipline of market forces in a market where long-term reputations matter, even when there is an implied federal safety net.

Summary and Conclusions

Regulation of OTC derivatives securities markets is clearly important to prevent the spillover effects of systemic risk and to preclude taxpayers from picking up the bill from their implicit guarantee to large financial institutions. However, the present and proposed rules for capital adequacy of derivatives are too simple. They are simple to implement, but inconsistent with modern financial economics and how these risks are correlated in practice. The proposed rules cannot readily incorporate new instruments, particularly those whose values depend on new underlying assets or indexes. The proposed rules would degrade the market for derivatives securities, thereby endangering a prosperous U.S. industry—one that provides essential risk-management products for a growing list of firms, and more importantly one that may easily migrate to a foreign shore.

One way to proceed that at least one Federal Reserve Board Governor is sympathetic to is to allow internal (i.e., bank) models to determine regulatory capital requirements.[9] While this may sound like asking the fox to guard the chicken coop, it would obviously respond to Edward Kane's regulatory dialectic, leap-frogging financial regulators onto the same page as the institutions they regulate. Moving in this direction would mark a truly innovative regulatory response to a truly innovative industry.

Professor Samuelson has remarked, if I'm not mistaken, that economics is less than a science and more than an art. This makes him feel that economics is fascinating, and he carries on with his studies. This notion of his has encouraged me to come here at the request of Professor Sato to discuss a subject on which I cannot possibly claim to be an expert. I was a student of law, not of economics, the sciences, or the arts, and I therefore am not in a position to speak of anything related to economics with theoretical precision. I hope that you will bear with me for this disadvantage. Having said that, I feel free to go ahead with today's topic, which is the Japanese economy, the bubble of the eighties and the recession of the nineties.

Everyone is keen to know what is happening in Japan today with its shifting political scenarios. Two days ago I discussed the possibilities for the future with a couple of members of the Liberal Democratic Party, and it appears our political turmoil may be resolved toward the end of this week. The current thinking is that there are three candidates on the table. One is Hata, the present Foreign Minister; the second is Takemura, who is the Chief General Secretary of the Cabinet, and the third is Watanabe, a member of the LDP. If Watanabe is nominated, coming out of the Liberal Democratic Party, he will bring some dissidents with him—probably somewhere between 60 and 80—but that's still a matter for speculation. Somebody said that it may be more like 40. If he is able to carry 70 or more, however, their number will outweigh the presence of the Socialists, which would provide a very stabilizing sort of anchor.

There is also talk of a general election if we cannot come to any more amicable arrangement. This would be one of the worst possible scenarios for us. LDP politicians were known for their secrecy and their hidden agendas. Nobody ever knew what was really happening behind the political scenes. Hosokawa and the coalition, on the other hand, are transparent, easy to read. Vague as his policies so far have been, filled with promises but lacking in any apparent substance, Hosokawa continues to enjoy enormous popularity simply because he represents such a different style of leadership from what we had in the past. He has brought a whole new atmosphere to government in Japan, and we worry that a general election will cut this new era short. We look to our three potential new candidates then, in the hope that the coalition government will succeed in its path toward stability and reform.

In discussing the Japanese economy, I need to return for a moment to 1985 and the Plaza Accord. It was after the Plaza Accord that the yen started to appreciate dramatically at the very moment the economy had begun to decline. Fortunately for Japan at that time, our industries were able to take full advantage of declines in both oil and import prices, which provided them with cheap raw materials and cheap energy when they needed them most.

Once the initial economic shakeup had settled, it appeared that the new level of the yen was going to remain steady for a while. The Japanese export industry was able to survive at the new level of exchange rate with the help of windfall profits that had accumulated during the period immediately preceding the Accord, when the yen was cheap and the U.S. government showed benign neglect for a stronger dollar.

Given this buffer, it was not so surprising that our industries were able to emerge in due course from the glow of the yen's sharp rise. Although some industries, especially the smaller ones with less international competitiveness, ended up in liquidation, the process was not as painful as we had anticipated because the assets that remained with them were still increasing in value. This story is in marked contrast to what is happening currently in the Japanese economy. For one thing, cheaper import prices are not performing their expected function, or are performing it too slowly to make a difference. Whether or not this is related to the growing share of service industries in the GDP or to the high cost of labor, maintenance, and infrastructure is not clear.

To return to our history, in February of 1987 the offshore discount rate was cut five times, from 5 to 2.5 percent. Meanwhile, accumulated wealth had reached a high enough level that people were starting to look into new areas of financial investing beyond traditional savings banks. Interest rates were liberalized. The demand for money by the public sector increased. The government and local authorities were actively borrowing from the capital market for infrastructure costs and Social Security, while private-sector borrowing became essentially inactive. This was the first time in Japan since World War II that the movement of interest rates appeared to be functioning properly, and market principles began to prevail. Many new financial commodities were introduced to the market. So-called securitization became financial, and the capital market became quite animated. Stockbrokers were creating a climate in which investors bought GDP growth and ignored price-earnings ratios as high as 80 in their investment decisions.

The low interest rate remained for a very long time, and the incident of Black Monday on Wall Street in October 1987 was one of the elements that caused our Central Bank to hesitate in raising the discount rate. Euphoria was created both in the financial and the real estate markets, and a similar environment in the United States and in other countries around the world served to fortify the Zeitgeist in Japan, too.

It can be argued now that we could have done something at that time to prevent the situation from reaching the extremes that it did. Nobody but the *Economist* in London gave warning signals against this general euphoria. The Bank of Japan increased the discount rate in May 1989 to 3.25 percent, but then Minister of Finance Ryutaro Hashimoto intervened and prevented it. Then a change of governorship of the Bank of Japan took place in December of 1989, enabling the Bank to increase the rate on their own initiative.

The official discount rate was increased five times from 3.25 to 6 percent during May 1989 to August 1990, in an attempt to tackle the apparent overheating of the economy. In the meantime the private sector's investment in production facilities was very buoyant during this period, with an 8.6 percent increase in 1987, 16.8 percent in 1988, 14.3 percent in 1989, and 11.4 percent in 1990. These figures reflect the slow effects of the change in discount rates under the high liquidity situation of the market. Moreover, warnings in the latter part of 1989 did not influence the investment decisions of the Bank of Japan in 1990.

Under these circumstances, the markets experienced for the first time a liberalization fortified by the abundance of money. They went on to play a go-go game. The masters of the game were ambitious young people who had no concept of the market's cycles of ups and downs. The prudence and the caution of the older generation was ignored. This aggressive capital investment was supported and facilitated by the new money created in the buoyant capital market at a very low cost. Our young investors believed that the average growth rate of 5 percent achieved over a four-year period reflected true potentiality for growth in the future, and made their investment decisions based on this expectation.

True growth potential must have already been down to

around 3 percent by this time, but buoyed by their euphoria no one was seeing clearly. Our present overcapacity situation was created in this way, and it has taken a lot of time and effort to remedy. It is now commonly acknowledged that the peak of this economic boom was reached around April 1991. Thereafter the economy started to decline, finally reaching the level of the present recession. During this period oil prices increased as an effect of the Gulf War, an additional blow to the declining economy. The Central Bank finally began reducing the discount rate in July 1991 and continued until September 1993 when the rate came down to 1.75 percent, the lowest in the Bank's history. Ultimately they were criticized for being too slow to act.

Now the recession has lasted for almost three years. GDP growth for the 1993 fiscal year was estimated to be around 0. This year's growth is estimated at about 0.7 to 1 percent by the majority of the economic research institutes in Japan. The government's estimate is 2.4 percent, but this would be almost impossible without some extremely aggressive government measures.

In the past two years the government has tried four times to stimulate the economy, in an aggregate amount of $430 billion. This figure includes public investment of $160 billion, and a tax cut of $53 billion. However, this did not produce the expected effect. One reason is that stock adjustment for equipment investment took an unexpectedly long time, and another is that the higher yen has inhibited an upward move.

The fiscal stimuli mobilized during this period were larger than those at the time of the Plaza Accord. Previously, the aggregate amount was 13 trillion yen, which included public investment of 7.5 trillion yen and a tax cut of 1.0 trillion yen. Public investment growth rate on a GDP or GDE basis was 9.3 percent in 1987, compared with 16.7 percent in 1992 and 14.4 percent in 1993. If you include the surplus in the Social Security account, Japan's fiscal balance was not so inadequate in the past. Recently, however, the OECD forecast a deficit of 2.4 percent in Japan's GDP in 1995, including the Social Security surplus. The recent hard line of the Ministry of Finance may be based on this or a similar forecast.

During these ups and downs of the economy, the banking industry has encountered many new phenomena. Securitization or dis-intermediation caused corporate clients to leave the banks and look toward the capital markets. Banks had to find new customers if they wanted to maintain an adequate level of credits, and they turned to the new, growing area of real estate financing. Due to the increasing value of real estate, the value of collateral increased as well while the battle was in progress. Hence, both banks and nonbanking institutions found that more credit could be extended on the basis of such increased value of collateral. They began to extend credit aggressively for 100 percent collateral value, thinking that real estate prices would go up indefinitely.

This of course turned out to be mere myth. Some commercial buildings in our large cities are 30 percent lower in value now than at the peak of the bubble, and loans were caught by this decline in the value of collateral. Most of the nonperforming assets of the banks are in real estate, and the viability of some of the nonbanking institutions will also depend on how they cope with their real estate loans. The banks have just closed their books on the 1993 fiscal year, and the figures are not yet available. To what extent disclosures will be made is also not yet known. Current speculation by the banking industry is that it will take three or four years for the major banks to clear up these problem loans.

Based on this hindsight, many things can be said. The surge in asset value was in fact one sort of inflation, and should have been treated as such. The BIS (Bank of International Settlement) rule of capital adequacy was handled very badly in Japan. We should not have included the unrealized gain on the securities portfolio as Tier Two capital. Production capacity should have been curtailed in proportion to the capacity created in overseas subsidiaries.

At present the issues of the trade surplus, the two-tier price mechanism between tradable and nontradable goods, government regulations, the iron triangle among politicians, bureaucrats, and industries, and the volatility of the yen rate are all on the table. It will be necessary for us, the Japanese, to cultivate a very strong political will to cope with these problems. The old, very pragmatic, political ideal of "catch up and surpass the West" is obsolete, and we need a new one closer to the everyday life of the Japanese people. If we are to succeed, we are going to need to focus on increasing the general standard of living and providing comfort for the aged in this aging society.

PAUL A. SAMUELSON

Earlier this year I attended a California conference on international finance. All the usual suspected experts were there, and if Robert Triffin were not dead he'd have been there, too. There was one surprise, though. Rip Van Winkle, beard and all, turned up at the first session. "What are you doing here?" Chairman Randall Hinslow asked. "I'm here to give the long view," Rip replied. Well, that is my function on this panel. I am here to give the long view, and I have the worry wrinkles to prove my competence. By the long view I don't just mean the long view back in history. I once heard a wise man say: "The future is longer than the present."

I can top that, and remember where you heard it first: "The future is even longer than the long past." There is only one history behind us, but there are many histories ahead. Those who don't know history are condemned to repeat it. So said George Santayana. When I quoted this to Harvard's Crane Brinton, he retorted: "Yes, and those of us who know history are condemned to repeat it with them."

Concretely, right now in 1994, Europe and Asia need economic stimulus while America needs to worry about overacceleration of our cyclical recovery. I like that. It is not that uniformity and consensus is boring. I could live with that and love it if what the whole world faced in common was brisk growth at full employment with virtual price stability and an eroding away of economic inequality. It is a common world pattern of instability that one must fear.

World War II was the watershed. Before 1939, the National Bureau of Economic Record used to measure pretty much the same business cycle all over the world. The Kredit Anstalt Bank failed in Austria, and not five miles away from here Manufacturers Hanover Bank closed its doors and set off an avalanche of 10,000 bankrupt American banks.

So it used to go most of the time. Before 1800 Britain began to pass through cycles of good and bad times. Each decade brought its bubbles of speculation, panic, and main-street business distress. As the industrial revolution spread—first to France and the Low Countries, then to North America, and eventually to Germany—the annals of business cycles trace a common international pulse. Of course, amplitudes varied and there were the inevitable regional leads and lags.

Certainly the adoption of a universal gold standard enforced a lock step on Argentina, Poland, and Manchester, England. Even today, when you look at the European Currency Union, you see how high unemployment is in France, Spain, Belgium, and other currencies recently pegged to the German mark.

By contrast with the prewar epoch, since 1946 America has repeatedly gone through its own extra business cycles while the Pacific Basin and the Common Market have experienced their own ups and downs. Why do I like that better? It is better because strength in American when Europe is weak works to moderate the average variability in both places. The Law of Large Number acts to make four independent regions have only twice the total variability of any one—where, by contrast, four perfectly correlated units will together have four-fold total variability and no halving of per-country volatility.

Let's be concrete. In mid-1982 Paul Volcker at the Federal Reserve fired up the American locomotive by well-calculated risk taking in the form of credit expansion. The German and Japanese locomotives were at dead center. Almost at once the Wall Street bond and stock markets felt the kiss of Prince Volcker's stimulus. The warmth spread to Main Street in Peoria and Gary, Indiana. And with small delay Nagoya and Düßeldorf shared in the American expansion. Even the domestic locomotives of policy chimed in as the Bundesbank and the Bank of Japan were reassured by favorable balances of trade.

That's history. I expected it would maybe repeat itself in 1991 when Alan Greenspan at the Fed was nagged into reducing U.S. short-term interest rates. Well, I am still waiting for the Japanese authorities to get their macro act together so as to bring an end to their quite unnecessary prolonged domestic slump.

Maybe the difficult reunification of Germany creates some genuine hesitancies there concerning a full court press against recession. But why should France and Belgium and Spain condemn themselves to double-digit unemployment just because Germany fears she has unification complications?

I ask why? You know why. That's what the Rules of the Game under the so-called Treaty of Maastricht dictate. Central bankers in London, Stockholm, New York, and Frankfurt were saddled by the mischievous Muse of History with the gold standard. Like Pavlovian canaries who beg to be locked back in their cages, modern savants of finance have put dunce caps on their own heads and asked to be chained together in the lockstep of a pegged-currency-parity schemata. We can leave to the give-and-take of discussion the next steps in world macro programming.

Although as an economist I lack the laboratory that my chemist colleagues at MIT possess, economic history has its impish ways so that life is never dull and always there are new lessons to learn and old ones to unlearn. By the caprice of how the dice roll, real growth in U.S. GDP turned strong six months ago. No mortal economist predicted that. No one? Almost no one. Franco Modigliani was an exception. But Franco is more or less immortal anyway.

I cannot believe that our luck must condemn Europe and Japan to imitate any new credit tightness here. But I have learned not to be a cockeyed optimist. It is not that I learned to be a dismal economist when I attained my Ph.D. degree at Harvard. Rather it is the case that I try to be a realist. To a fault, I hate to be caught wrong.

PANEL DISCUSSION

WILLEM H. BUITER: I have a question/comment for Richard Levich, which is that any regulation of the derivatives market would have to be at a global, not a national level. The market is completely footloose. It could be anywhere. And with the Internet, it can be everywhere. What we are seeing, you refer to the fact several times, is competition, intended or not, between national governments to attract the derivatives business. This could lead to competitive weakening of regulation and would in my view call for something similar to what the BIS has done in the Basel agreements for bank capital adequacy repeated at a global level to prevent a kind of nefarious competition to the lowest common denominator, which is, I think, a real threat with this business.

RICHARD LEVICH: Let me say a couple of things about that. One is that I fully agree that regulation, to be effective, would have to be implemented at a global level. But I fear that some of our own domestic legislators may not be so aware of that. After the 1987 crash, ideas about trading halts, changing margin requirements, and transaction taxes were proposed for our own markets, even though they might not apply to other countries. That scares me, because at least half of the centralized futures market activity is presently in the United States.

I take your second point exactly as said, that this indus-

try is very footloose, so that if we impose regulations that are costly as we've seen in other examples (the Eurocurrency market and the Eurobond market were the two that I mentioned), the activity could go elsewhere very quickly.

And regarding regulation, one of my themes was that there is plenty of demand for self-regulation and for capital requirements that are sensible within the private sector.

It strikes me that one of the approaches taken recently by commercial banks and securities firms, is to try to bring market regulators (especially those at the BIS) into the fold. By teaching regulators what they would teach their own personnel, the kind of regulation banks and securities firms get doesn't simply drop out of the sky and doesn't bear any relationship to industry practices, but in fact is heavily influenced by people within industry itself.

TORU KUSUKAWA: Willem Buiter mentioned something in his talk about a dirty float. The concept was very familiar to me, because I was one of the members contributing to that dirty float. I was actually in Düβeldorf, in West Germany, conducting all sorts of interventions. As Richard Levich discussed, at that time it took 24 to 48 hours for Japan to make deliveries. But this dirty float concept, well, I'm just wondering. Journalists say nowadays that some American officials high up in Washington want to see the Japanese yen much stronger and so on, but with that sort of notion, the exchange market will react. It reminds me of George Soros doing his magic act with the English pound, which he withdrew from the market until it came back to a certain level.

"Talking up" or "talking down" the exchange rate can still be possible, especially for us. If there is any notion that the yen should be higher or lower, the markets react. But if this sort of notion was made by somebody with direct or indirect authority to decide the intervention of the Central Bank, the market would naturally take it for granted that this is an open declaration that a certain government is not going to make any interventions. This creates distortion or overshooting of the rates, as we have seen in the past six months or so. So I'm just wondering, with this concept of the dirty float, if it may have something to do with the present situation in the exchange market, although the exchange market itself must function as properly as it can. I really wonder about the integrity of the market right now.

Willem Buiter also mentioned that Japan should keep full employment. I very much doubt this is possible, because of the hollowing out of our industries that is taking place at this time. We have this very expensive Japanese yen. A lot of production lines are moving out of the country, with Southeast Asia and Mainland China being prime targets for these transplants.

The last time we tried such an exodus we made a serious mistake by not shipping the products back to Japan. They were sold in the places they were made and in other foreign countries, so that we would not need to make any adjustments to our production capacity. This time, because of the very high cost of wages and infrastructure, I think the overseas Japanese subsidiaries will be shipping their products back to Japan. If that happens, it means the curtailment of the production line in Japan altogether—a potential source of major unemployment.

Also, although we are seeing the present trade surplus rise to 3.3 percent of GDP, it's likely to come down to, for argument's sake, 2.3 percent—down 1 percent in terms of GDP. We are trying very hard to increase the GDP by 1 percent, but if we have a trade surplus adjustment lowering the GDP then it could be harsh to Japanese industry. That may cause some unemployment as well.

PAUL A. SAMUELSON: I thought at the beginning there was so much agreement here that there would be nothing to find to disagree with. However, I have managed to find some at least minor points.

First, I think that the conservatism of the Japanese bureaucracy is a very important fact. It is not an alibi which passes muster at seminars of economists, but it is a valid excuse. If Japan is unwilling to have a deficit and treats any public-sector deficit as an evil thing, if investment opportunities are very low in Japan and are going to stay very low because of past excessive investment, and if there's a Central Bank that is determined not to let the real interest rate go down as low as possible, it is asking too much of a laissez-faire system for it to be able ever to cure itself. The only way Japan is going to solve its problem, if at all, is through the international sector.

Just a few weeks ago we had a conference here sponsored by the Japan-U.S. Center, a very good one, on Eastern Europe. We learned that a country like Ukraine has 16 times the steel capacity per person that the great steel producer, the U.S., has. This is all being maintained like a Potemkin village production out of printing money. No jury of sensible economists could say, "Give blessings to that." There has to be a massive readjustment of resource use in the selfish interest of the Ukrainian people for the future of their country.

The same thing I think is likely to be true of a Japan that has been in a long Schumpeterian phase of having technological productivity growth in excess of that of its principal rivals, and I believe there has to be a deployment of Japanese resources, as Schumpeter himself would have told you. What a Japan could do twenty years ago, a South Korea could do ten years ago, a Malaysia could do yesterday. I don't think that Japan has gone through enough of an identity crisis yet to have worked out the details of this deployment.

Now I believe eclectically that there ought to be public-sector, infrastructure buildup, spending (which will shock the bureaucrats) along the lines of your own Mayakawa Report of earlier years. That would solve part of the problem. I think a deepening of capital in Japan at lower and lower real returns can still elicit some increase in capital formation there. I think Japan will have to move out of what has now become routine manufacturing, and of course you know that. It was easily done when Japan was growing well. It was called the hollowing out of Japan, the outsourcing. But when all of that is done, if it still would be dynamic comparative advantage for Japan to be doing the saving it wants to do and provide those savings to the rest of the world, which still has a need for capital formation, I want to outline what I consider to be the most desirable way for that to come about, although not what I realistically think will come about.

There is no reason why this outsourcing should necessarily be associated with Japanese imperialism. There is no reason why Japanese corporations, which have generated Schumpeterian temporary profits, should not use those profits to go abroad. I don't speak with forked tongue. It's the same advice I gave the Norwegian government. Instead of spending on marginal health and education schemes in Norway, I said, "Invest abroad." That doesn't mean that we have to have a new set of Vikings marching across the world.

So far the Japanese have not shown great comparative advantage in foreign investing. It's true you can buy three New York skyscrapers for the price of one Tokyo skyscraper, but mostly you've been sold lemons, everywhere in the country. The four great Japanese brokerage firms were a little bit like Keystone Kops in their investment behavior. This all could have been avoided. Goldman Sachs would have handled their account. The efficient way is to have it all end up with Vanguard. Low loads, low expenses. Let the impersonal capital market, free of nationality, allocate the monies abroad. This also will keep

Japan on very friendly terms with everybody. People in Southeast Asia will love the Japanese, saying, "There's no threat here at all." (I'm speaking a little bit unrealistically perhaps, I admit.)

Now to tie up a very small disagreement with Professor Buiter. He warned us we shouldn't mistake competitiveness for deficits, and we shouldn't. But we should have a micro concern that a nation like the United States, which was a leader early in the game, is losing its uniqueness as others imitate it. There should be concern here for the country as a whole not to lose consumer surplus from international trade. This scenario is in the cards under the strict laws of dynamic comparative advantage if country after country acquires new technical proficiency in precisely those sectors of American activity that historically were the leading ones.

We should be concerned enough to do something about that. This concern could show itself in subsidizing Cal Tech, for example—I won't mention MIT. We also need a realistic exchange rate, one that helps to make the best use of our micro aggregated labor markets. I don't think it's good economics to say that General Motors' competitiveness is different from U.S. competitiveness because General Motors can disappear but the U.S. can't and won't. We're not talking about General Motors' management or General Motors' stockholders—we're talking about their resources, which previously were spread around the U.S. in the auto industry, and what their new best use should be and to what degree at a realistic wage level General Motors can maintain a sustainable comparative advantage in the automobile industry here.

NOTES

1. For the first time, annual volume on the 47 non-U.S. exchanges exceeded that on the 15 U.S. exchanges. *Directory and Review, Futures and Options World* (1994), p. 7.
2. Ibid., p. 11.
3. Ibid.
4. Ibid., p. 35. FRB (Federal Reserve Board), FDIC (Federal Deposit Insurance Corporation), OCC (Office of the Comptroller of the Currency).
5. The OCC has published guidelines making it obligatory for banks to ensure products are appropriate for customers. (Ask yourself whom this regulation is protecting.)
6. Frederick G. Fisher, III, *Eurobonds* (London: Euromoney Publications, 1988), p. 10.
7. Edward M. Kelley, Jr., "Developments in the Dollar Payments System," remarks delivered at the International Symposium on Banking and Payment Systems, Washington, D.C., March 10, 1994.
8. See, for example, Paribas Dérivés Garantis, a subsidiary of Compagnie Financière de Paribas, described in *Structured Finance* (Standard & Poor's, November 1993), pp. 91–92.
9. Susan M. Phillips, "Derivatives and Risk Management: Challenges and Opportunities," Remarks at the Conference on Financial Markets, Federal Reserve Bank of Atlanta, February 25, 1994.

CHAPTER 6

International Investment: The Japan-U.S. Dimension

April 20, 1994

INTRODUCTORY REMARKS

ROBERT KAVESH: We have several distinguished guests in our audience today. I worked for a few years for the Harvard Economic Research Project. Professor Leontief was my dissertation adviser, and it is a pleasure to have this Nobel Prize winner here with us. It was more than 40 years ago, when we were young, that I worked with him. Let me also introduce Will Baumol, one of the truly distinguished economists in this country, and, if I may say so, my own choice for the next Nobel Prize. Lastly, I would like to welcome Michael Schiff, who teaches here at the Stern School—former Chairman of the Accounting Department and one of the true pillars of the School.

Our speakers today include Fujio Cho, President and CEO of Toyota Motor Manufacturing, U.S.A., Inc.; my colleague from the Stern School, Professor Joshua Livnat, a widely published author and current Chairman of the Department of Accounting; and finally, in the baseball season and every season our cleanup hitter, Professor Paul A. Samuelson.

FUJIO CHO

Four years ago Toyota Motor Manufacturing (TMM) was awarded the J. D. Power top quality award as the best quality plant in all of North America. The next two years TMM finished second and third. Then, in last year's survey, our team members recaptured the top award. This year we hope to win our third Gold Plant Quality Award. For all of us at TMM, winning this award is like winning the World Series or the NBA Championship. When you think of the fact that almost all of our production team members, 100 percent of whom are Americans, had no prior experience of working in a manufacturing environment, let alone in an automobile plant, this accomplishment is simply extraordinary.

Just a little more background on TMM. We added engine production, an additional $300 million investment, in 1989. Three years ago we experienced our first major model change. In 1992 we became the world's sole source for Camry station wagons, and last year TMM became the sole manufacturer of the Camry coupe. Today Kentucky Camrys are exported to more than twenty countries all over the world, including right-hand drive models to Japan and the United Kingdom.

TMM continues to grow. Just about a month ago the first Camry sedan rolled off the new line in our $800 million expansion plant. When the expansion plant reaches full production, our capacity will be 400,000 cars per year. Starting this fall we'll be building the Avalon there as well, the brand new Toyota flagship car. This will be a huge challenge for us. It's extremely rare in our business to start a brand new car in a brand new plant.

V-6 engine production will also begin this fall in TMM's power train expansion facilities, which will be completed this summer. With all of these expansions, Toyota's investment in Georgetown, Kentucky, has grown to more than $2 billion. Our total employment will reach 6,000 by the time we reach full speed.

Certainly Toyota's investment in Kentucky has been a success story from our point of view. However, what does this investment mean to the local community, to the State of Kentucky, and to the United States as a whole? That's more difficult to answer, but maybe a few key statistics will help. First off, TMM has a payroll of $235 million annually. That alone is significant. More comprehensively, Dr. Charles Haywood of the University of Kentucky recently published a study on our plant's economic impact. According to his calculation, the direct and indirect effects of TMM have created some 20,000 jobs in Kentucky. The same study forecasts that the number of Kentucky jobs generated by TMM investment will grow to over 22,000 by 1996, once our expansion reaches full capacity. Dr. Haywood also estimates that TMM's economic impact has created more than 60,000 jobs in the U.S. as a whole, and that the U.S. impact will reach 92,000 jobs by 1996.

Now it hasn't all been perfectly smooth sailing. We have

moved a big production facility into a fairly small town, and I worry about our impact on Georgetown traffic and schools. But we are doing everything we can to minimize any adverse impact on my new home town, and hopefully most citizens of Georgetown would agree. Overall, I firmly believe Toyota's investment has been clearly beneficial for the community, the State of Kentucky, and the United States as a whole.

In addition to our economic impact, I'd like to believe that our presence here has been helpful in another way. It is much more difficult to quantify than economic impact, but I think that Toyota has another contribution to make, in the area of technology transfer. Since technology transfer is sort of an overused phrase these days, let me be more precise. I'm really talking about spreading the ideas of the Toyota Production System. We call it TPS for short.

Let me explain. Historically, the Japanese auto industry took a different road in its development from that of the American auto industry, and until very recently the flow of information and technology had always been one way—from the U.S. to Japan. The Japanese auto industry has learned tremendously from the Americans, as well as from such splendid teachers as the late Dr. Deming. As I remember, throughout most of my career at Toyota we were learning from and at the same time trying to catch up with America.

The younger audience may find it hard to believe, but Japan in the fifties and through most of the sixties was a poor country. Toyota as a company was no exception. We just didn't have any money to spare, yet we felt we had to catch up with the world's richest nation and the world's best auto makers. It was out of the question to pour money into R&D or new state-of-the-art equipment.

What we did, like many other Japanese manufacturers, was to take what we had, be it equipment or human resources, and try to figure out the best way to utilize them to achieve maximum efficiency. In so doing Toyota eventually developed the Toyota Production System, which is now recognized throughout the world as the "lean production system." It was this lean production system that made it possible for Japanese auto makers to eventually build high-quality vehicles at low cost.

The American auto industry has been a great teacher for the Japanese industry. As the student, Japan learned so well as to reach the point of equality. In Japanese thinking this is the highest compliment to an excellent teacher. This same philosophy tells the student that he owes his teachers a debt of gratitude in such a situation. Just before I left Japan to head the TMM project I had a meeting with Eiji Toyoda, then Chairman, and Dr. Shoicho Toyoda, then President. They wished me luck for the success of the TMM project, and asked me to do something that would be beneficial to the United States while I was working in this country.

As I mentioned, the Japanese auto industry is indebted to the American auto industry, their teacher. Both Toyodas were telling me that it was time for us to repay all these obligations. Of course my first priority was, and still is, to start up TMM smoothly and to make it grow into a mature and profitable automotive plant. But while I have concentrated on the TMM operation I have also always been on the lookout for opportunities to repay our obligations to the U.S. In fact we've been able to do some of that through our day-to-day operation.

As I explained before, our team members had almost no experience in automotive manufacturing when first hired. We had to train them from scratch. Toyota believes that the Toyota Production System is the best production system we could have. Naturally we are trying to practice TPS in Kentucky, so we trained our team members in such key TPS elements as "standardized work," "kaizen" (continuous improvement), "kanban" (inventory cards), and "line stop system."

With some modification to suit American culture, TPS has taken root in our plant. It is still in the growing stage to be sure, but I believe that our team members will eventually reach the level of their counterparts in our Japanese plants, probably in five years. I consider TPS to be the "know-how" or technology of the manufacturing industry, and the fact that our American team members are learning and mastering TPS means that there is a kind of technology transfer taking place in Kentucky.

TPS also has implications for our suppliers, as you might suspect. When we began our production here in the United States, we started out with a policy of Americanization of parts and materials wherever and whenever possible. TMM's local procurement started with $70 million purchased from 92 suppliers in 1988. With much effort by our purchasing department, TMM's U.S. procurement in 1994 will reach $2 billion purchased from more than 200 suppliers in 32 states.

As you are probably aware, Toyota's purchasing operation has been somewhat different from the "traditional" American way of purchasing parts and material. It took a while for our American suppliers to become accustomed to our ways and to find that our way has merit for them, too. We probably go much further than most American auto makers in our relationship with suppliers. For example, TMM established a "Technical Support Group" in our purchasing department to support any of our suppliers who request assistance in improving their product quality and/or their productivity. This group has been in existence for about five years.

Another example of Toyota's effort in "technology transfer," which expanded the idea of technical support although not directly associated with TMM, is the Toyota Supplier Support Center, or TSSC for short. It was established in Lexington in 1992 with the sole purpose of assisting any American manufacturers who were interested in improving their manufacturing operations. Incidentally, TSSC doesn't charge any fees for their support services. Without any publicity, they have received 145 requests so far. In the first year they helped 23 companies. Five of them completed their requirements and eight more companies were added, so TSSC is working with 26 companies this year.

One TSSC-supported company reports its productivity rising 450 percent! Their lead time shrank to one-fifth, and the inventory was reduced to one-tenth of what it was before working with us. Since we can't give in-depth help to all interested companies, we are now trying to satisfy more people by giving seminars on the Toyota Production System (TPS). I understand that many of the Big Three plants have begun to use the lean production system in their operations. It may be the reason why TMM gets numerous requests from Big Three companies to tour our plant and discuss various aspects of TPS. In 1993 there were 37 visits by Chrysler, GM, and Ford involving over 200 people. I feel that accepting such visits is another way to repay our obligations, and we will continue to welcome them.

So far I've talked about TMM's economic impact and our effort to repay indebtedness through technology transfer. We can talk more about such efforts as being a good corporate citizen, but since my time is limited I'd like to turn now to an issue that has recently been of deep concern to us, the constant threat of government trade sanctions. First, let me explain. Toyota has been blessed with tremendously friendly treatment by the people of Kentucky and Americans in general. TMM's Kentucky team members are a great bunch of diligent, world-class workers. My neighbors in Georgetown and central Kentucky have been kind and supportive of me personally, and the same is true for the 60-plus Japanese on loan from Toyota Motor Corporation.

What concerns me, however, are a series of legislative threats and comments made by politicians on the federal level. Such bills as the "Trade Expansion Act of 1992," also known as H.R. 5100, and the federal legislation entitled the "American Automobile Labeling Act" are frequently introduced to the U.S. Congress, and many of these bills tend to discriminate against companies like TMM. I guess the intent is to get back at Japan for any perceived barriers there against U.S. exports. But I fear the sponsors of these bills don't really consider the potential impact on the Kentuckians who work at TMM, or for that matter on thousands of Americans who work at other so-called transplants.

For example, the American Automobile Labeling Act will apparently require us to place labels on all new passenger vehicles disclosing such information as the percentage of value of equipment that is considered to be of U.S./Canadian origin for a car line. One of my major concerns is the phrase "a car line." Toyota imported about 30 percent of Camrys sold in the U.S. in 1993. So the Camry's domestic content, for the car line, will show a much lower figure than the ratio TMM has actually achieved in our Camry. In effect, I'm afraid that the label will give a distorted impression that TMM is only a "screwdriver operation."

This is quite unfair for our Kentucky team members, who are working hard machining engine parts, stamping most of the major stamped parts and components and making plastic parts such as installment panels and bumpers. Along similar lines, *Automotive News* recently reported that many senior members of the Clinton administration "valued Big Three jobs more than transplant jobs." Again, I guess the reason is they don't like Japan's trade practices. But Kentuckians at TMM say they deserve better than to be treated as second-class citizens.

Our American team members do not understand this treatment from their own government. As for myself, I wish that they would just allow us to concentrate on building high-quality cars to serve our American customers. After all, a big reason the Big Three have made so much progress is due to competition. At any rate, as the trade friction between Japan and the U.S. gets heated I worry about both sides seeming now to be centering on our differences in customs and business practices, which leads to even more criticism of each other. Certainly, there are differences. After all, they are two different cultures. These differences need to be systematically and scientifically analyzed. I strongly feel that both the Japanese and the American sides need to base their discussion and negotiation on facts and reason, rather than on stereotypes and guesswork.

Maybe there is a way those of you in the audience who are in academia could help. One way might be through scientific research into these business practice differences so that the arguments surrounding them are based more on facts and reason.

JOSHUA LIVNAT

I guess the topic today is going to be mostly cars, so it would be appropriate to talk about international misconceptions about cars by telling you a joke that comes from my country, Israel.

This is about the Israeli who hosts his Texan brother. When they get up in the morning the Israeli brother, who is a farmer, takes the Texan out of the house and says, "Do you see that tree?" The Texan says, "Yes." "That is the boundary of my farm." The Texan looks at him, all amazed, and he says, "Look. On my farm you get into the car, drive for three days, and you don't get to the end of it." The Israeli brother looks at him pitifully and says, "Yeah. I had a car like that, too, but I managed to sell that lemon."

I think people have a lot of misconceptions once they start going across international boundaries. Given my training as an accountant, what I would like to do is not talk about macroeconomic effects such as the frictions between the U.S. and Japan, but instead try to identify how the U.S. investor, or for that matter any investor, should go about making international investments—whether in foreign countries or in the securities of foreign countries.

What I would like to do is talk about free cash flow as the basis for investment. This is from a paper I wrote with

Ken Hackel, who is a money manager in the U.S. Using this principle of free cash flow, he now manages over $1–3 billion with pretty good results.

In terms of the general way that investments are made, I think there are three distinct stages. The first is screening. In the U.S. there are currently about 11,000 stocks that one can choose from. I once figured out that if I had to analyze each company on my own, it would take probably a lifetime to go through just one cycle of analyzing all these companies adequately. So what we have to do is cut down the universe and concentrate on just a few companies.

Let's say we screen a large database that contains information about companies and then limit ourselves to a subset of those companies, say a list of 50 stocks. We then conduct an in-depth analysis of these 50 stocks and decide which ones to invest in. This is going to be the investment portfolio. Suppose we end up with a list of 30 companies that we will ultimately invest in. The third step in the investment process is to decide about the selling criteria: When would we sell the portfolio holdings?

Why does it make sense to invest abroad? I think there is no dispute that foreign economies have their own business cycles, and business cycles, for good or bad—I personally think it's good—still affect the stock market. By keeping this in mind, the individual investor is able to diversify away the effects of the economic cycles in any one country.

We also find out that foreign equity markets react differently from domestic markets to news items. Let me give you a couple of examples. One of them I witnessed as a student at the Stern School, in its previous location downtown. We had a conference on options, I think, and a news item came in that President Reagan had been shot. No one knew his condition, and it took literally less than two minutes for the hall to empty out. There were two pay phones in the lobby. People started bidding on these pay phones, up to $200 to make a phone call so they could execute some trades. As a poor Ph.D. student at the time I had an urge to try to arbitrage by suggesting to one of these people that they walk up two floors to my office and make a phone call for only $50, but that would have been unfair—so I let the market take its course.

Meanwhile, in Thailand, the elected government was ousted by a military coup. The Thai stock market on that day went up by $1\frac{1}{2}$ percent. Just think about the major differences in these two countries. In the U.S. you have a major impact just on announcements that the President was shot, with full uncertainty about his condition. It turned out in fact not to be such a major item. In Thailand the whole government is abolished by military coup, and nobody is affected. So foreign markets react differently to news.

Of course, we would also like to invest internationally because of risk reduction. What we see is that capital flows extremely fluidly now from one country to another. Years ago international transfers of funds were a major endeavor. Today you do it electronically and the money is transferred within seconds. We also have instantaneous information transfers. You go abroad, get into your hotel room and turn on CNN, and it's just like being home, right? And you have fax machines that transmit information within seconds again anywhere in the world. Tremendous improvement.

What problems do we see with foreign investments? First of all, we don't have standardization of information. We have differences involving quantity of information, timing of information, and quality. As an accountant I should probably point out that accounting information differs across countries. Each country has its own accounting rules, and the accounting rules don't agree and are not consistent with each other. Somebody comes and tells you that it's always good to invest in low-priced earnings multiple. That may be a good strategy in the U.S. but may work poorly in a country like Japan, where, unlike their U.S. counterparts, corporations try to minimize their accounting income because that income is subject to taxes and the two coincide.

We also point out that the flow of information changes. In some countries, like the U.S., quarterly information is sent out to investors. In other countries the flow of information to investors may be semiannual or even annual. We find out that in Japan, for example, corporations are required to report to stockholders only twice a year rather than four times a year. The joke—and this is only a professional joke, so don't take it too seriously or too literally, but the joke is that in Germany if you want to delay your annual reports all you have to do is say that your accountant was sick and you can get an extension for a few months.

We know that timeliness also affects the flow of information across countries. In the U.S. you're required to publish financial reports to stockholders 45 days after the quarter's end. In Australia, which is a modern, English-speaking country, you're required to file your annual report within 120 days after fiscal year end. The median company in Australia reports to the stock authorities 127 days after its fiscal year end, which means that more than 50 percent of the Australian companies are late in reporting. Timeliness, again, may be important. Investors process information differently, and of course we know that enforcement is radically different across countries.

What could one do in order to make some sense of the reports that appear in different accounting languages using different accounting information? What we suggest is using a common yardstick: Free cash flow. There are some technical requirements for such a yardstick. To begin with, we would like to define free cash flow as all the cash that one could withdraw from a business without affecting its future growth. You want to make sure to maintain the level of growth sales that you currently experience. Anything above that can be taken out of the business.

We have our own methods of estimating it, but let me show you what happens when you invest using this measure of free cash flow. Take three portfolios: First a portfolio based according to the free cash flow concept; then a market index, composed of an equally weighted average of all the companies in the database (about 4,000 non-U.S. corporations); and lastly, a portfolio adjusted to the size of the company and its relative book-market ratio. We find that the portfolio based on free cash flow consistently has higher returns than the other two portfolios, either the market portfolio or the portfolio based on similar size and book-to-market.

We feel very comfortable with this definition, and think that it may be one way of going beyond trying to compare accounting reports that use totally different accounting methods across countries—a common yardstick, common denominator if you want, or common measure that you could use in order to screen a large database and pinpoint companies for international interest.

We backtested this strategy from 1987 onwards. It's interesting that no Japanese firms passed our screens as portfolio candidates in 1987 or 1988. The first time we started seeing some Japanese companies appearing on our screen was 1989–1990 after the large drop in prices in the Japanese stock market, which in some sense gives us some reassurance about the process that we use.

PAUL A. SAMUELSON

Today America seems to be growing well—maybe even too well. At the same time Japan still seems to be stagnant in overall GDP.

Today America's stock market, influenced by a bond market weakened by a post February 4 move of the Federal Reserve toward tightening of credit, seems queasily to be in a possible retreat from a durable bull market. By contrast, Tokyo equities have behaved better in the last year than the American market.

When real estate prices in America were soaring and Wall Street stocks were generally rising, Japanese investors were cheerfully recycling their export surplus toward our shores. Skyscrapers, golf courses, and joint ventures with U.S. firms were eagerly embraced by Japanese insurance companies, banks, pension funds, and nonbanks. It is said that after being burned by many such investments, Japanese money managers have begun to cut their losses while refraining from throwing new good money after bad.

One supposes that this change in asset preferences—from animal spirits or rational recalculation—helps explain why the dollar continues to depreciate against the yen right in the face of rising nominal and real interest rates here at home. Of course it does not help that (1) Japan's multilateral surplus continues to swell in dollar terms; and (2) her bilateral surplus with America continues to swell in dollars. (One must be reminded that, as the yen appreciates vis-à-vis the dollar, both of those current balances could begin to diminish when reckoned in terms of the yen. American jingoists can thus sometimes accuse Japan of contriving a worse surplus at the same time that Japanese jingoists can point to a worsening yen-reckoned surplus.

Just nine days ago, here at NYU, our symposium touched on these matters. An informed expert from the Fuji Bank complex explained why, in about four years' time, the banking system in Japan might be able to accumulate enough earnings to work off its bad real estate assets. The key, he suggested, was to use as a Japanese-American dictionary the Mitsubishi Bank, the only Japanese bank to prepare reports for American shareholders protected by the SEC. One could translate the Mitsubishi Japanese accounting reports into American terms by comparing them with the Mitsubishi American accounting reports, and by applying the same ratios to other banks' available Japanese data one could hope to estimate their meaning in standard American accounting terms.

I found that a bit reassuring. Actually I had feared things might be a bit worse—which would have been ominous for the future of foreign investing and the instability of the floating exchange-rate system. The prospect of a dollar that has fallen to below 100 yen in price would be daunting if a still further overshoot could be rationally feared.

I wish that the reform coalition government in Japan had the will and the power to dismantle on a grand scale all barriers to trade. That would be a good thing for the vast majority of the Japanese people. Any harm to particular vested interests—such as rice farmers—could be partially or wholly compensated for, and still the nation would be ahead.

This plea for freer trade from the Japanese side is not because I expect that such a reform would cause America's current deficit with Japan to evaporate or even drop substantially. I do not believe that 100 percent free trade would greatly alter the present composition and volume of either of the two countries' exports and imports. What it would do is add to economic welfare in both places. And, with protection out of the way, noneconomists could see what economists understand to be the following truth: With Japan being a high-saving society facing limited investment opportunities at home, and with America being an affluent, low-saving society with a still chronic fiscal deficit, one must expect the normal equilibrium state to involve a chronic Japanese surplus on current account and a chronic American deficit on current account.

The world is in need of the capital formation that Japanese thrift can help finance. As the Japanese population ages, the future fruits of assets owned by Japanese corporations and families will be increasingly needed at home. And all this can be effectively sustained under present-day floating exchange-rate mechanisms of the post-Bretton Woods type.

Now what would be implied by a successful development along the lines I have sketched out above?

I want to describe two alternative scenarios. One of them will come as no surprise to most observers. The other may at first seem more novel. My purpose is not to come out for one of these scenarios and to come out against the other. Actually, it could be advantageous to embrace a mixture of both of them, letting further evolution determine the rights of the blendings. There is no need to decide on either/or, no need to make up one's mind at this time for or against either.

Scenario 1 declares that if Japanese savings are spreading into capital formation in different parts of the world, then it has to be Japanese corporations and managements who do the managing of these investments. What Japanese militarism did badly in her prewar imperialism in China and Far East Asia, now Japanese multinational corporations can try during peacetime to do well and in a way that is popular with the host peoples who are the recipients of Japan-financed capital formation.

Scenario 2 divorces the process of providing investment funds for foreign investment from the process of managing them. In this view, savers opt to be rentier owners of bonds and equities. To understand this process, only contemplate the many hundreds of billions of dollars saved by Americans for their future pensions. Their money managers entrusted with these funds do not manage productive corporations and do not try to perform Schumpeterian acts of innovation. Instead they make judgments concerning which venturesome and experienced corporations are worthy of being invested in.

To be concrete, when I was a writer for *Newsweek* I wrote a famous column called "Advice to a Sheik." Having Saudi Arabia or Kuwait in mind, with their vast and new oil revenues, I counseled: "Invest much of your surplus abroad rather than create an inflation at home at too fast a pace of attempted development. Instead simply buy a portfolio of Standard and Poor's 500 Index. Hold it in Switzerland if you like. No other investment can be so liquid on demand and so well-diversified."

I was wise beyond my time. Many of the Kuwaiti takeovers in places like Spain have been simple disasters. The skyscrapers and golf clubs bought in America by Japanese have often been lemons. The record in America of the four great Japanese brokerage firms has certainly been nothing to boast of. I suggest that Scenarios 1 and 2 both deserve reflection.

PART THREE

Sanwa Lecture Series

CHAPTER 7

Recent Economic and Financial Trends Affecting Japan and the United States

March 8, 1993

INTRODUCTORY REMARKS

MARTI SUBRAHMANYAM: We are today at the crossroads in both the Japanese context and the U.S. context in terms of economic policy. After a long period of growth both countries have been plunged into a period of recession, out of which the U.S. is only recently emerging and Japan is yet to emerge, or perhaps has just begun.

Both countries are contemplating major revisions in their fiscal policies, although in somewhat different directions. In both countries there are doubts in many quarters about the efficacy of social policies. In the United States we've seen a lot of discussion of health care issues. In Japan there has been a lot of attention paid to the regulation of financial markets. We will see further developments in both countries I suppose over the course of the next few months, as their new policies take shape and evolve.

Our first speaker is Professor Merton Miller. Professor Miller is one of the founding fathers of modern financial economics and has made contributions to virtually every area of economics and finance. A Nobel Laureate, he is the Robert McCormick Distinguished Service Professor at the University of Chicago.

MERTON MILLER

When I got the invitation to be a lead-off speaker talking about Japan-U.S. relations under the Clinton administration I couldn't help but think of a famous document in the Widener Library at Harvard University. It's an exam paper written many, many years ago by the great American humorist Robert Benchley, and the exam he was called on to write was, "Discuss the Canadian-American Fisheries Treaty of 1876 from the viewpoint of one of the participants." He wrote it from the point of view of the fish, and that's the position that I want to take today. I want to talk about U.S.-Japan relations from the point of view of the fish, namely, the consumers in both countries. Nobody pays too much attention to them, or as much attention as they should. All our emphasis, I'm afraid, is on the producer's side.

So let me first talk about what I think these trade relations mean for U.S. consumers, and here I think the Clinton administration has been giving very mixed signals so far. That's not necessarily a criticism. It's a new administration, after all, and it's still not clear who really speaks for it on matters of international policy. The administration hasn't gotten down to specifics yet, but I'm part of a group very much afraid that their motto may well be one that I once saw on a bumper sticker, which I'll edit for this audience. The bumper sticker said, "The hell with price and quality. Buy American!"

We're soon going to get some tests of where the administration stands on a variety of these issues. There's this much discussed matter of the vans, for example. Are they to be considered trucks and pay a 25 percent tariff? Or autos, at $2\frac{1}{2}$ percent? Also looming in the background are threats on the part of our automobile companies, or at least some of them, to invoke the antidumping laws. Those laws could do a considerable amount of damage to American consumers.

Let me add right away, however, that I am not praising the previous administration in contrast to the Clinton administration. Many anticonsumer moves of this kind were made by the Bush administration. The only difference that I see is this, and it may be an important one. When the Bush administration did it, it was with a sense of guilt because they at least felt that they should be strongly pro-free trade. I'm not sure how deep the free trade instincts of the current administration run, but I'm certainly not condemning them out of hand. I'm saying that in the next few months we will see.

For the Japanese side of the equation, I really think that things are going to be looking up. The Clinton administration, whatever its policies may be about letting imports in, is certainly going to be pushing very hard on Japan to get its barriers down and possibly even to elevate the yen. Although this will cause a lot of screaming, it may ultimately be good news for Japanese consumers. The more access and the easier access they have to world commodities, and to U.S. ones in particular, the greater the benefit to Japanese consumers.

I especially want to point out one area in which I believe the Clinton administration will eventually pound sufficiently hard on the Japanese authorities to get them to do something—prohibitions on rice imports. I always tease my Japanese friends about how much luckier we are in America than they are in Japan. I happen to be a great rice eater. I love rice. I not only eat Japanese rice, which is good (I even like the sticky variety as well as the regular). It's great rice—but so is arboreo rice from Italy, which you won't find in Japan. So is basmati rice, from India. That's great stuff, too. So is Thai rice. All these magnificent rices from around the world, and for some reason for all these years Japan has prevented her own people from eating them. To me it makes absolutely no sense, and I think we will help the Japanese get rid of these restrictions.

Now rice is one of my hobbies. Futures markets is another one, and on that I hope that the Clinton administration will pound on the Ministry of Finance (MOF) a bit—in fact a lot. In fact I hope they will pound MOF into the ground. I have several complaints about MOF that I want to talk about, but I'll mention two where I think gentle pressure from abroad can be a help. We have first of all succeeded in getting the MOF to allow American firms to enter the brokerage industry in Japan and give some healthy, well-needed competition to that closed cartel. Such are the facts of life over there, however, that although an American firm could join the Tokyo Stock Exchange, it still could not tap the local Japanese retail market very well. Japanese firms, understandably, have a big advantage in the local market. But foreign firms could at least take advantage of futures trading, which, as a result of pounding from the U.S., MOF finally had to permit.

Unfortunately, in one of these post hoc/ad hoc situations, no sooner had MOF allowed U.S. firms to engage in substantial amounts of futures trading than the Tokyo Stock Market went into the tank. And of course MOF, like anybody else would under the circumstances, said, "Aha! You see? We told you this was going to happen if we allowed futures trading." Well, there's a simple way to show you that the fall tanking of the stock market in Japan was not in fact due to futures trading. Look at Taiwan. The fall there was every bit as prolonged and as intense as in Japan, and there was no futures trading whatever.

Futures trading had nothing to do with the case. But MOF couldn't seem to understand that, because here were these American firms making huge quantities of money while the stock market was going down. MOF figured they somehow had to be selling; that they had to be violating the well-known Japanese taboos against selling stocks. But they weren't. The arbitrage involved had them all buying Japanese shares and selling futures. What they were doing, as I've tried to explain in some recent papers, was arbitrating commissions, not prices. MOF had set such an artificially high level of securities commissions that American firms who had the know-how were able to utilize these new developments to — "hollow out" I believe is the phrase Professor Horiuchi used—to hollow out the Japanese stock market and switch the business over into the futures market.

I think MOF understands this now. But what it's doing, and where I hope we can exert some pressure on them, is trying to expand MOF's influence, baneful influence in my opinion, not just at home but around the world. The Nikkei futures contract is traded in Singapore on the Simex Exchange, and when MOF put out all kinds of restrictive rules in Japan the business just moved en masse from Osaka to Singapore (where MOF pursued them). The Japanese went to Singapore and tried to persuade them to adopt Japanese restrictions, and now they're putting pressure on us, the Chicago Mercantile Exchange, to also make some changes in the way we trade the Nikkei Index.

I hope that the pressure that our government can exert on MOF will help free the Japanese capital markets and make them into modern markets. I always feel Japan is a twentieth-century economy, or soon to be twenty-first, with a seventeenth-century regulatory structure. MOF-style regulation is no longer appropriate for a serious country, as Japan surely is.

Let me conclude on this note. Whether MOF can be reformed or not, I don't know. One reason our regulators don't do some of the things MOF does, like try to support market prices, is that our regulators know that it won't work. That's bad enough. They also know that if they try and it still doesn't work, they're going to get blamed for the failures.

Now MOF is being blamed for the failures all right, but what can you do about it in Japan? In the U.S., if the regulators fail they know they'll be kicked out of office. But there is no opposition party in Japan, and as a result there are no penalties on MOF for its conspicuous and embarrassing failures in trying to support the stock market. Now you asked me to be provocative. What do you think?

MARTI SUBRAHMANYAM: Professor Miller, as usual, has been very forthright in his views. I should mention a couple of facts that may be of interest. First of all, Professor Miller is on the Board of Directors of the Chicago Mercantile Exchange. The other fact that may be of interest is a curiosity, that one of the earliest financial futures exchanges that I know of was in Osaka in, I believe, the late eighteenth century.

MERTON MILLER: Even earlier than that: 1640.

MARTI SUBRAHMANYAM: 1640, was it? And it was actually a market that traded futures and forward contracts on rice warehouse receipts. So in a sense this is not a new thing for Japan, and perhaps the Japanese authorities will heed Professor Miller's advice.

MERTON MILLER: Let me just mention that I was in

Osaka during my last trip to Japan and I placed a wreath of flowers on the site of the first futures exchange in the hope it may revive.

MARTI SUBRAHMANYAM: I turn to the next panelist, Professor Masahiro Kawai, who is visiting us from Tokyo University. Professor Kawai is a prominent Japanese economist, whose research interests range from the economics of commodities markets to issues of macroeconomic policy. He is on the faculty of the Institute of Social Sciences at the University of Tokyo.

MASAHIRO KAWAI

Professor Miller talked about pounding the Japanese market, putting pressure on Japan, and he sort of suggested that because of the lack of effective opposition parties in Japan, the United States can play the role of an effective opposition party. I have to say it's very sad and unfortunate from the Japanese viewpoint that so many things have to be done by opposition parties outside of Japan. The situation has to change.

I believe that certain things are in fact going to change. Professor Miller talked about rice. I want to touch on that issue as well. I wanted to talk about macroeconomic issues, microeconomic issues, and international trade and finance issues, but given the time constraints I have maybe I'll touch on just certain aspects of macroeconomic issues and then I want to talk about international trade, the finance aspect particularly.

Now as everyone knows, the United States is in the process of getting out of its recession. Japan is still in the middle of a relatively severe recession, and many people say that the current recession in Japan, which is sometimes called the "Post Bubble Recession" or the "Heisei Recession," is the most severe recession Japan has faced since World War II.

Actually, if you take a look at statistics, that's not quite so. From the 1970s we have had three recessions, including the current one. The most severe was from 1974 to 1975, after the price shock. At that time, if I can give you some numbers, real output declined very fast. From peak to trough, industrial production declined by almost 19 percent. But this time the decline is 7 percent. At the time of the price shock, real GDP or GNP declined very close to 3 percent—this time from 0.4 to 0.6 percent.

Now in 1992 real output is still declining, and we don't quite know when it's going to stop. But given the stimulus by the Bank of Japan, which has reduced the discount rate six times from 1990, and given the fiscal stimulus that the Minister of Finance is now undertaking—and the Minister of Finance is trying to undertake further fiscal stimulus—I don't think this recession is going to last very long.

Some people have called the current recession structural rather than cyclical, but I disagree. It is very cyclical. Japanese business firms accumulated too much capital stock in the late 1980s given the macroeconomic environment. At that time there was a sudden surge in the confidence of a lot of Japanese firms in business sectors as far as the future of the Japanese economy was concerned. They invested a lot in capital equipment and the stock price somehow went up and then suddenly started to collapse. Too much capital was accumulated, and too much debt incurred by the business sectors. Now the Japanese economy is trying to take care of that problem, and after this stock adjustment phase I believe that the economy will come back.

The tensions between Japan and the United States result

from the opposite directions of the two countries' economies. The U.S. economy is growing, the Japanese economy is still down, and that's widening the trade imbalances between the two countries and is one of the sources of economic tension between them now. But I don't think this sort of cyclical tension will last for a long time.

Now on microeconomic issues there are many things to be done, but I'm going to skip this part, with one exception, which is the need on the part of the Japanese agricultural authorities to be firm on their future agricultural policy. The problem with rice in Japan is internal, not caused by the pressure from abroad. The agricultural sector is structurally depressed. No young people want to continue farming. No young people want to inherit the farmland from their parents. There is really no future in Japan in terms of rice farming. Structural change, policy change, has to take place, and I think it will.

Moving to international trade, in the Uruguay Round of the GATT negotiations the role of rice from the viewpoint of Japan was not the most important impediment, but was still an important issue—not for the United States, not for Thailand, not for Vietnam, but for Japan. It's about the future of Japanese agriculture.

Congress passed some years ago a resolution to the effect that Japan does not import even a grain of rice. That's the official policy. But actually some grains of rice are being imported. Lots of rice is being imported in the form of processed rice as well, so actually that policy is not being maintained anyway. But still, that's the official policy. Now some factions of the LDP, our Liberal Democratic Party, are suggesting that Japan should open up its rice market. Some members from the Socialist Party are now raising up a solid voice as well, and consensus is emerging in Japan to open up the rice market.

The question is not really whether the Japanese rice market should be exposed to foreign competition, but rather to what extent Japanese consumers should support their rice farmers. I believe some consensus will be reached, has to be reached, before the current GATT Uruguay round is concluded. People believe it's going to be concluded some time this year and Japan has to move, and it is after all in the best interest of Japan to move in that direction. Japan cannot continue to have a depressed agricultural sector.

We cannot really talk about Japanese trade policy independent from U.S. trade policy. Japan is heavily dependent on the United States for trade, for investment, and in many other areas. Her choices are heavily influenced by U.S. trade policy.

I will summarize my remarks by pointing out some options that Japan can take with regard to its international trade or trade policy. Maybe government bureaucrats and some people may be upset when Professor Miller says that the United States will pound the Japanese government and apply pressure to open up the market. Actually the government has been doing just that. But anti-U.S. feeling is rising in Japan now, and it looks very unfortunate. As Professor Miller pointed out, trade frictions are not the frictions between the entire nation of Japan versus the entire nation of the United States. They are frictions between a set of producers in Japan versus another set of producers in different countries, and consumers have their own very different interests, different from those of the producers in their own country. We have to understand that.

Still there is a feeling in Japan that Japan should not depend too much on the United States in terms of the export market, but should move her weight more toward Asia. That's one direction that Japan can take. Actually Malaysian Prime Minister Butir proposed the East Asian Economic Grouping (EAEG) idea, and Asia is now considering that possibility.

That's one possibility. However, I believe first of all that if Japan's move toward Asia is accompanied by opening the Japanese agricultural market to Asia, that could be a step toward freer trade from the viewpoint of the world as a whole. If Japan moves more toward Asia in its trade investment and at the same time maintains a kind of military arrangement (the U.S. presence), free trade may not be that hard from an economic viewpoint. It may even be quite useful, just like a NAFTA agreement could be useful for the world as a whole. But of course there is a political concern here. It's quite unrealistic. I cannot spell it out now because of time.

Another direction, an opposite direction, that Japan could take would be to completely integrate Japan with the economy of the United States and North America by forming a U.S.-Japan Free Trade Agreement, or by joining the NAFTA. Now in order for this to be viable the Japanese economic system would have to be equalized, to be level with that of the United States, establishing a level playing field across the Pacific. The United States for its part would need to accept the existing savings/investment imbalance with Japan, so that if large trade imbalances continued they would have no political consequences. But these two conditions seem quite difficult to realize. In the short run then this path may also be unrealistic.

The most realistic path would be to use an expanded Asia Pacific Economic Cooperation (APEC) forum, to include all of North America, Japan, the Southeast Asian countries, China, Australia, and New Zealand. To free up trade by using such a forum of loose economic cooperation would be the most realistic option for Japan, and the Japanese government is indeed pursuing that option. The only problem is that it might lead to a two-bloc world economy, Europe versus APEC. Japan would benefit a great deal by multilateralizing her trade relationships with the rest of the world; thus, APEC would need to include Europe as well. That would be the most realistic and least costly way to involve Japan in liberalizing the international trading system.

MARTI SUBRAHMANYAM: I was interested to hear your reference to Japan's growing interest in the rest of Asia. On a recent visit to Japan I heard a presentation on China, and was struck by the differences in perspective between Japan's view of China and that of the United States. This is a topic I would like to come back to later. Let me now turn to the next panelist, Professor James Tobin. Professor Tobin, whose name is I'm sure familiar to all of you, is a Nobel Laureate. He is one of the stalwarts of Keynesian economics and has influenced national economic policy from the days of the Kennedy administration up to the present.

JAMES TOBIN

If you look at the world economy these days I think you will see that the Group of Seven advanced countries—and especially the Group of Three among them, Japan, Germany as the key country in economic policy for Europe, and the United States—is not doing very well. The world wasn't doing very well in the eighties. It looks like the nineties are not turning into a very good decade either. The administration of the world economy by this group of central bankers and leaders hasn't been very successful in terms of economic growth, prosperity, and unemployment.

It looks to me like Japan and Germany have been fighting the wars of the 1970s for twenty years now, with rather disastrous results for their respective economies. If you look at the unemployment rates in Western Europe you see lots of double-digit rates, and right now you see lots of negative growth rates for industrial production and GDP. Japan of course doesn't have unemployment in the same sense as Europe or the United States. But especially relative to the sustainable growth rate of Japan, which I should suppose is 4 or 5 percent per year, they certainly haven't been doing very well. I think a lot of this poor performance is linked to the prevalence of monetarist and other sorts of noninterventionist macroeconomic views among the leaders of Japan and Germany.

The United States, as it was in the 1980s, is a bit out of synchronization with the rest of the G-7 or G-3. That's good for us if we have a recovery when they're still in recession. But of course the depressed condition of the rest of the world is an important handicap for United States recovery, because it's bad for our exports, our trade balance.

Let me turn more specifically to the United States and the Clinton administration's program. The Clinton administration has known for a long time, even before the election, that it faced a dilemma between, on the one hand, economic stimulus to restore employment in the United States and get the economy moving again, a short-run business cycle problem, and, on the other hand, deficit reduction to deal with the longer-run problem of the inadequacy of American saving and investment.

Clinton's policy crystallized when the administration got into office. The advocates within the administration favoring first priority for deficit reduction really won the President's approval. The emphasis of the program presented on February 17, 1993 to the Congress and the public is really on a several-year program of deficit reduction. The higher taxes and expenditure cuts proposed in the program will have actually begun already if the program goes through as presented, in the sense that the proposed tax increases—the income tax increases, not the energy tax increases—are supposed to be begin retroactively from the date of passage back to the first of this year. That may not last of course in the actual legislation.

The earlier idea was for a stimulus to dominate the first couple of years, to be followed by an austere deficit reduction package. The stimulus part has been cut way back until it's almost nonexistent, apart from the investment tax credit (ITC), however, which is sure to be enacted but which will only last for two years. There won't be any stimulus even from that source then after 1994.

So at most we are going to get a deficit reduction that is less than a deficit-increasing stimulus in the first year only, fiscal 1993, and that's going to be of an order less than half of 1 percent. It's hard to imagine that that's going to make a great deal of difference in the macroeconomic outlook.

I think the upshot of all this is that the ball has been passed to Alan Greenspan, the Chairman of the Fed, and his colleagues. If we're going to have a strong recovery, then it's really going to be up to him and his policy to be more activist, more aggressively expansionary, than the Federal Reserve has been accustomed to being recently, especially in the last four years. Fiscal policy is going to be leaning against the wind as it is, so it would be undesirable and certainly unnecessary for the Federal Reserve to be leaning against the wind as well in accordance with their ordinary practice during recoveries.

Let me emphasize we have a long way to go to achieve a complete recovery. The recent statistics on GNP growth and one month's recent statistics on employment growth are promising signs, and it may be that we already have sufficient stimulus and sufficient optimism to keep the economy going without help. But we have about eight million jobs to create to attain an unemployment rate of $5^{1}/_{2}$ percent in 1996, the rate that we had before the four years of growth, recession, and stagnation from 1989 to the present. Eight million jobs—that also means we would have to make up a gap of around 5 percent between where we are now and what the gross domestic product would have to be for the economy to produce that kind of lower unemployment rate.

Since the normal growth of the economy needs to be around $2^{1}/_{2}$ percent per year just to keep the unemployment rate unchanged, to make up a shortfall of 5 percent through four years we're going to have to have growth every year on average between $3^{3}/_{4}$ and 4 percent per year. Growth of 3 percent is nothing to write home about. Growth of 3.8 percent, such as we had in the fourth quarter of 1992, is something else. If that were to continue, it would lower the gap. But that's going to be against the employment-reducing effects of the austere deficit reduction program, the defense cuts and tax increases in the program, and also against the downsizings, structural adjustments, and permanent layoffs that are being made by many American companies at this time. Recovery is not in the bag, and our fiscal policy as now planned is not going to do much to help.

Now let me just remind you that this administration on coming into office inherited from its predecessors at least six really difficult economic problems in the economy. One is the recession, high unemployment, and the stagnation of the economy for the last four years. The second is that for a longer time than that we've had not a cyclical problem but a long-run, secular problem, not a demand shortage but a too-slow rate of growth in our productivity, in our ability to produce goods and services, mirrored in a very disappointing and upsetting way to Americans as a downward trend in real wages, at least in take-home real wages.

That's the longer-run problem, to which the third problem, the persistent deficit in the federal budget, is related insofar as the remedy for the second problem, the slow growth of productivity, might entail a higher rate of investment and saving. Fourth is the health care cost explosion, which will bust the budget in the latter part of this decade regardless of what happens as a result of the present deficit reduction package. In addition to the present deficit reduction plan there's going to have to be another one to accompany health care reform. Otherwise the first plan will be overwhelmed by the growing explosion of Medicare and Medicaid costs in the last part of this decade.

Fifth, we have the backlog of needed public investment of all kinds—infrastructure, education, and so forth—that has built up in the last twelve years. Something ought to be done about it. The deficit reduction plan addresses some, though not all, of this. I think that's a good aspect of the plan, but people are saying, "Well, if we're going to try to reduce the deficit we shouldn't use any of the savings or new taxes for those programs. They should all be put into deficit reduction." Finally, sixth is the growth of inequality of income and wealth during the past twelve years. A little something is being done about it in tax and other reforms that are being proposed.

That's a big menu of problems that nothing was done about for twelve years, and suddenly Clinton is expected to solve them all. Some patience and understanding might be called for.

I'm not going to comment any further at this time on trade policy, other than to say that the macroeconomic developments overseas, especially if we have a recovery and the other guys don't, may exacerbate the trade problem by increasing our deficits in trade and increasing the Japanese surplus, and that's probably a big danger as far as protectionist temptations in the United States are concerned.

MARTI SUBRAHMANYAM: Our next speaker is Masahiro Yoda, General Manager of the New York branch and Managing Director of the Sanwa Bank. Masahiro Yoda has extensive experience as an international banker, having served the Bank in London, New York, and San Francisco.

MASAHIRO YODA

I am very pleased to have the opportunity to speak today with such a distinguished group of economists. I feel like a different species sitting here, and to avoid a fierce argument later with the other panelists I would first of all like to speak briefly about the history and professional activities of Japanese banks in the United States from my experience as an international banker for thirty-two years—eleven years in the United States, seven in England, and the remainder in Japan.

Americans are familiar with Japanese companies like Honda, Toyota, and Sony. Unfortunately, since the majority of customers of Japanese banks here are large corporations (with the exception of such places as California where Japanese banks conduct retail banking operations), there is little opportunity for the general public to understand the activities of those Japanese banks that have become a part of daily life in the United States. I would be happy if my remarks today presented the realities of the U.S.-Japan relationship in its financial-economic aspect. Later, of course, I would like to comment on the U.S.-Japan relationship in the financial community and the international situation.

To begin, I will provide a brief review of the expansion of Japanese banks into the U.S. economy. The history of that expansion covers less than forty years, so it is not an old story. To arrive at its present status, that overseas expansion went through four stages, beginning in 1950. During that first period of time Japanese banks gradually opened offices, mostly in New York, for the purpose of helping Japanese trading companies doing business in the U.S. As a result, most of the business was related to U.S.-Japan trade, such as using U.S. dollars for foreign exchange transactions.

The second stage of expansion began in the 1970s, when Japanese banks grew rapidly through the medium- and long-term syndication loan market in New York and in London. Another development during that period was a shift in lending by Japanese banks from Japanese companies doing business in America to American companies. The third stage of expansion was in the 1980s, and was a business evolution for Japanese banks in the United States to reach their new level. They were able to begin a period of complicated expansion and business diversification. For the financial community, in the midst of deregulation, the 1980s was a time of driving demand for total funding in reaction to increased mercantile position and trading activities. However, the best developments of this era were the swaps and options. Japanese banks were also actively participating in these business trends.

The 1990s will mark the fourth stage of business activity for Japanese banks accompanying the economic downturn in the United States. Japanese banks, along with their American counterparts, saw the defaults on the credit they had extended for LBOs and real estate transactions during the period of go-go banking in the 1980s. Also, there were new management issues for Japanese banks from various sources.

As Japanese banks enter the fourth stage of expansion in the 1990s, they face a turning point. I'll mention three factors for this impending change in direction. First, the relative competitiveness of the Japanese banks declined after the burst of the so-called bubble economy, mainly because of the sudden increase in troubled assets in real estate lending. This resulted in serious pressure on bank earnings, and rating agencies began to scrutinize Japanese banks and to downgrade their ratings. Although most of the Japanese commercial banks retained their A ratings, the rating gap between Japanese banks and their American counterparts was shrinking.

Second, there has been a strengthening of banking regulations by the financial regulatory authorities. In addition, the capital requirements by those authorities have been strengthened recently. As you well know, the stock market in Japan hit the bottom in late 1989, and continued to hover at that level. Banks were faced with an unfavorable situation for capital rates. Their lending activities will continue to be restrained accordingly. Japanese banks are pursuing calculated expansion, but it has become difficult. That's why it is essential for us now to closely review our business strategies and the organization strategy to determine the direction of future activities in the U.S. market.

Now it appears that the new government is going to

implement policies that will raise the level of competition while securing the evenness of all conditions of competition. However, excessive government involvement and regulation might jeopardize the relationship of cooperation and competition between the United States and Japan. We have enough regulation and control by the government, as Professor Miller has already mentioned. In the financial industry, too, excessive regulation is becoming a problem. Sources of funds for financial institutions have decreased not only for Japanese banks in the United States, but also for American banks. There is a concern that government involvement and regulation will hinder the smooth flow of funds to American industry.

Of course that doesn't mean that we are against opening up the Japanese domestic market. We welcome deregulation. Unfortunately, imitating the Securities Act of 1933, Japan created a very strict division between the securities business and the commercial banking business. There are moves in the United States currently to lessen this division, however, and hopefully Japan, affected as she is by attitudes in the U.S. government, will follow suit. We look forward to seeing the division between the securities business and the commercial banking business lowered, and we would welcome pressure from the United States on the Japanese government to open or deregulate the Japanese financial market.

As far as the Clinton administration is concerned, it is in the process of implementing its policies. Hopefully the results will revitalize the American domestic economy.

Japanese bankers certainly hope that the allure of the U.S. market, one of the few markets in the world that is open and dynamic, is not diminished. We would like to help coordinate, if we can, the relationship between the U.S. market and the Japanese market in the financial community.

I hope this account has contributed to your understanding of Japanese banks and finance.

MARTI SUBRAHMANYAM: Next is Richard Zeckhauser, Frank Ramsey Professor of Political Economy at the Kennedy School of Government, Harvard University. Professor Zeckhauser has made extensive contributions to the field of economics research.

RICHARD ZECKHAUSER

I want to comment briefly on five areas: (1) the people and proclivities within the Clinton administration; (2) patterns of Japanese and U.S. investment; (3) political developments, particularly in Japan, because I think this will influence Americans' perceptions of Japan; (4) the changing military balance of power, which I think will affect relations between the two countries; and (5) the world's industrial landscape.

To begin with people and proclivities, it is important that the Clinton administration is more populated with lawyers than any administration we've had recently. The President and Mrs. Clinton are both lawyers, Mickey Kantor and Ron Brown, who are both vitally concerned with trade policy, are both lawyers; Robert Reich, who is a powerful influence on the President in economic affairs, is a lawyer.

I think lawyers think about problems differently than economists do. They're more pragmatic, they don't have a strong ideology one way or another. I think they tend to deal with cases, focusing less on precedents and principles than economists might, and I think you should bear this in mind when you try to predict what the Clinton administration will do. I'd suggest that if you look back four years from now and try to figure out what has gone on, there will be a less clear pattern than for many other administrations that picked their battles.

Economic relations between Japan and the United States have perhaps received too much attention recently, and patterns of investment that at least contribute to trade flaws have received relatively too little attention. In Japan, 1 percent of domestic sales are made by primarily foreign-owned corporations. In the United States that number is 10 percent; in Germany it is 18 percent. These patterns of investment, I believe, are very significant both as a signal and also for their influence on patterns of trade.

Let me just give you one other set of statistics about the flow of foreign direct investment. In Japan from 1985 to 1989 it totaled $400 million a year; in 1990 it was $1 billion; in 1991 it was $2 billion. In contrast, the flows from Japan were $17 billion, $22 billion, and $20 billion—somewhere between ten and forty times greater than the flow into Japan. (Japanese investment in the United States was $51 billion, $29 billion, and $14 billion during these years.) So what we see is Japan making dramatic investments overseas and foreign countries making tiny investments in Japan. However, the total U.S. foreign investment as of the end of 1991 was still somewhat larger than that of Japan.

There's an interesting question as to whether these patterns will be able to persist if Japan changes its own political landscape, as I suspect it will. It's no secret that Japan wants to play a more significant role in world affairs. There has been much discussion about Japan's assuming a seat on the Security Council in the UN and more generally playing a major role in security-related issues throughout the world. Any such effort will put Japan through some very difficult debates, as I understand it. As Japan debates revising its constitution, as the issue of political reform becomes more important in Japan (as it has in the United States) and should political parties realign in Japan, which could happen in part since the Soviet Union is no longer an external threat, my guess is that America will get a somewhat richer understanding of Japan than the current image of "the people who make Toyotas and Hondas."

Aside from the political arena, I see major shifts occurring globally in terms of military influence. The principal area where the Clinton administration hopes to cut expenditures is the military, and one of the easiest ways to do that would be to bring our troops home and reduce our defensive role abroad. I think we'll be doing that in Japan, and to some extent in Europe as well. It's much more acceptable, after all, to close bases in Japan than to close them in Florida. Widespread American troop withdrawals, however, will lead to a bit of military uncertainty throughout the world and particularly in Asia. I believe that Japan will step into this new scenario and expand its military forces to some extent, making the U.S. and certainly the Asian countries uncomfortable. Meanwhile Japan will be observing China, just next door—probably the most dynamic economy in the world today and a potential military threat as well.

For the past twenty years I would say the U.S.-Japan relationship has been frozen. Although economic rivals, the threat of the former Soviet Union to both countries kept us on the same side in almost all issues of world affairs. With that mutual threat gone, I think U.S.-Japan relations over the next 20 years are going to need to be redefined.

I believe the industrial landscape has a lot to do with the way the U.S. and Japan will compete in the future. Our primary problem, "we" being the United States, is that we're not investing enough either in general investments or even in R&D. We contribute about 1.4 percent of our GNP to industrial R&D; Germany contributes just under 2 percent; Japan is at 2.2 percent. This deficiency is going to be a long-term problem for us.

A critical question both for the United States and Japan is what type of firm is going to best equipped to compete in the twenty-first century. I think that's an open question. In the U.S., I guess the leading firm of the past 25 years (but not continuously over the last five years) was IBM. Before that, our leading firm was General Motors. Both companies were vertically integrated industrial giants spread around the world—and both at the moment are basket cases.

If you asked what are the two most successful large firms in the United States today there would be many candidates, but I would select Intel and Microsoft. Very different in their style of operation and in the way they make their products, they are both horizontal firms: They attempt to sell their products to others in industry. Neither attempts to produce its own computers or use its products in some other field. Japanese firms in general, certainly all the largest firms, are still very heavily vertically integrated.

It may be that U.S. firms and Japanese firms are different in nature. It may be that IBM and GM were just unlucky, or it may be that industrial production in the twenty-first century requires a different style of firm. I don't know which corporate structure is best. I do think that conditions in the economy change significantly over 20- and 30-year periods, and whichever type of firm prevails, the industrial picture is not going to remain as it appears in 1993.

In conclusion, I think that Japan's reputation is going to rise in the United States for a variety of reasons that have nothing to do with trade issues. As an American who has visited Japan several times I realize that most Japanese are knowledgeable about the United States, and I'm embarrassed to say that most Americans know virtually nothing about Japan. I think this will change, that Japan will rise on the American radar screen. Rising too high on the radar screen of the Clinton administration, however, may be a source of regret—I'm sure our own pharmaceutical industry, for instance, would have preferred less attention from the administration over these past few weeks. On the economic front, I don't think that trade will be the only friction. I think there will be more attention to issues of investment, and to the extent that trade is a friction I think that it will be dealt with on a case-by-case basis rather than more broadly.

I think that Japan will be flexing its muscles more on the international scene, with some reluctance: To the extent that it does there will be significant disagreements between the U.S. and Japan, something which has not happened since World War II. Japan and the U.S. will vote different ways on the Security Council, and people will be upset. I see Japan's military strength becoming a concern, and I think both countries will be ambivalent about this issue. Finally, I believe that the ability of foreign nations to invest in Japan will prove to be of significant economic concern for the next decade.

PANEL DISCUSSION

MARTI SUBRAHMANYAM: I would like to hear comments now from our panelists, and then we will open the discussion for questions from the floor.

MERTON MILLER: I have two very brief comments. First, just a little warning to Professor Kawai and his colleagues about extrapolating past Japanese behavior into the future. Remember that the demographics are changing again, and that's a very important element in the picture.

For Jim Tobin, I have some reassuring news. I believe that Clinton will not only be reelected in '96, but after him Gore and after him Hillary (maybe even before Gore). I agree with Jim that Clinton won't solve the unemployment problem. It may even get worse. In fact I expect that it will get worse during his administration. But that didn't stop Roosevelt. Roosevelt was reelected four times, and he was never able to solve the unemployment problem—and he incidentally had a very long period of cheap money policies going with him.

Clinton will be reelected because he's rediscovered the same strategy that Roosevelt did, and it's a very effective one. See, as a non-Keynesian I don't worry too much about the deficit. I don't even look at the deficit. I look at the fraction of national resources that are being taken by the government and used to provide services, and I see this going up. It's already going up under the Clinton administration. Now it's true, as Jim suggests, that they're going to finance some of that by taxes, but it's not going to be taxes on Clinton's supporters. It's going to be taxes on what are called the upper-income groups. This is exactly the same trick that Roosevelt used. I think it's a very effective one, and I think it will work.

JAMES TOBIN: It's just a matter of history. Economic growth in the recovery that started in 1933 was double-digit in real terms. It was 10 percent per year in Roosevelt's first term, and the unemployment rate was reduced from 25 to 14 percent. There was still a lot of room left before what happened in the second term of course, and the mobilization for war, but there was a substantial recovery occurring.

MERTON MILLER: It didn't seem that way then.

JAMES TOBIN: Yes, it did. I'm not going to go after Mert's political forecasts about the election, but I don't think unemployment will be worse in 1996.

MASAHIRO KAWAI: Regarding the Japanese economy, I would just like to clarify that I did not mean to suggest that it will continue to perform indefinitely as it has in the past. We know that Japanese society is aging. In the first twenty years of the next century, say by the year 2025 or something, about 20 percent of the Japanese population will be above the age of 65. Obviously this is going to have an effect on the basic economic behavior of Japanese consumers, as savers. What I was trying to say was that I don't think either the expansion of the Japanese economy in the 1980s or the current recession have anything to do with demographic factors. So over the next 20 or 30 years people's consumption and savings behavior will certainly change, and this is going to cause alarm on the part of our bureaucracy because the Japanese are going to save less. But that's where the Japanese economy will be affected.

MASAHIRO YODA: I'd like to comment on the Japanese contribution to international affairs. There is a lot of talk about changing the constitution in Japan, and recently there is a lot of talk about whether Japan should send its troops overseas. These are very, very difficult issues. Since World War II Japan has been transformed into such a peaceful country that none of the Japanese people today have any actual sense of what it means to get involved in war. I have a little different mentality. Maybe I have lived too many years in overseas countries.

I hear a lot of talk about changing the constitution. I should be very much for it. I feel it's time for Japan to do something to be more involved in international affairs, not just in terms of military power. In addition to the Communists, the Socialists, and the elderly, powerful LDP leaders are very much against changing the constitution and would limit the Japanese contribution to international affairs. But I do not think we can continue to just give money and never take any action.

As for the opening of the rice market, which Merton Miller discussed in his talk today, it is a very, very symbolic political issue. I would hate to see my name appear in some newspaper saying that the Managing Director of Sanwa actually supports opening the Japanese rice market to overseas.

MERTON MILLER: I'll take the blame.

MASAHIRO YODA: I don't eat much rice myself, but it's ridiculous to reject the import of rice. It's just a symbolic issue, and I don't think the LDP will do too much about opening the rice market in Japan. As a consumer I do hope that there will be pressure from the U.S. government.

MARTI SUBRAHMANYAM: I think Professor Miller and I will make up for your deficit in rice consumption, Mr. Yoda.

RICHARD ZECKHAUSER: I think rice consumption is relatively unimportant. I think it would be very good for America, particularly if we're worried about anything coming close to trade parity, to stop dealing with rice, which has unfortunately become such a symbolic issue, and worry about a variety of other issues.

On the election returns I'm not going to try to second guess Professor Tobin and Professor Miller as to whether Clinton will get reelected, but I will make the observation that the less President Clinton worries about getting reelected at each stage as he moves through policy, the better it will be for the U.S. economy and for Japan. People spoke a lot today about the difference between short-term and long-term perspectives of economic performance, looking at corporations. The same thing may be true vis-à-vis countries, especially if there were some way that Clinton didn't have to worry about having his policies rejected. I would like to insulate President Clinton from reading the next day's poll results in terms of formulating economic policy. The same thing was true of the Bush administration, the Reagan administration, and every administration before that. But I hope that President Clinton worries less about his reelection than the people on this panel.

MARTI SUBRAHMANYAM: Let me ask the panelists a question that has been on my mind and perhaps on the minds of others, and that is about the virtual stagnation in real income of a large segment of the middle classes of this country over the last two decades. This is an issue which, as an observer and as an economist, I have to resolve in the context of a world where we have trade agreements like NAFTA, the emergence of Eastern Europe, and the growing importance of China. How can the average American worker, or for that matter the average Japanese worker, maintain his or her standard of living in the face of growing wage competition from people in other countries whose productivity has been going up much faster?

MERTON MILLER: I don't think damage is being done to the middle class at all; it is the people at the bottom who are in fact competing against imports. What can be done about that? It's not as simple as saying, "Pour money into education." We've poured huge amounts of money into education. Something is dreadfully wrong with the way our educational system works, and I don't know what it is.

JAMES TOBIN: I think our problem is basically that the

rate of productivity growth in the economy has been too slow for a long time, not just recently but beginning back in the mid seventies, and that would be a problem even if we were a closed economy. Real wages would be declining, or at least not rising. We have some redistribution within as a result of trade and the competition of low-wage workers throughout the world. We have some redistribution within the labor force, at the apparent expense of members of our labor force who had noncompetitive high wages in the first place, such as in our automobile industry, and we're not going to restore that kind of advantage.

But one has to remember that other countries are not going to give us products across the board without some recompense, and our problem is not that we're not further ahead on the balance of trade, but what terms we have in the balance of trade. If the terms are bad, that's just a reflection in a financial context of the failure of our productivity, which is something we have to remedy both by investing in education, and by R&D and higher general investment over a long period of time. It's not something that's going to happen very quickly. We are a lot more efficient in many ways than those other countries, including Japan, especially in the production of nontraded goods and services.

MERTON MILLER: That's one of the nicest things I ever heard you ever say about our economy.

RICHARD ZECKHAUSER: I don't think there's all that much we can do. I think that if you go back to the 1950s or 1960s to give Professor Tobin his due, which may have been the heyday of American productivity, growth, and prosperity, we had large numbers of people working in highly paid manufacturing jobs who were less skilled than their counterparts overseas with nowhere near the access to the technology and capital that we had, and over the long run these people were bound to lose some competitive edge. In addition, our educational system has gotten worse. It's just accelerated that trend.

American productivity in most industries is still higher than productivity around the world. I think that a trend has developed during the eighties that will continue during the nineties, which is basically that our technological élite will do extraordinarily well, and one of the questions is whether we can pay the people who are toward the bottom end of our population enough to make them competitive. If we can, they'll do great. If we can't, they're going to do poorly.

I want to disagree with one point here. Everybody says that in the United States people aren't maintaining their standard of living. I think that's not true. I think if you appropriately correct for product quality, the American standard of living is going up. Anybody who compares 1960 cars with 1990 cars can see that they've dramatically improved. We could engage in a lot of protectionism, but we would end up driving down our standard of living with higher prices and lousier products. I don't think that's a particularly smart thing to do. I think that it will help some people over the short run but it will clearly hurt them over the long run, and I don't think that very many economists would disagree with that point of view.

MARTI SUBRAHMANYAM: I agree with you. I was just quoting a sort of widely held perception.

RICHARD ZECKHAUSER: Unfortunately the only people who listen to economists are other economists.

MARTI SUBRAHMANYAM: I was just wondering if there's a different point of view on this in Japan, because Japan is going to be put in the same situation, though perhaps from a different angle. What is the Japanese response to this issue? You have a billion Chinese who are now becoming more and more technologically adept and are going to really compete directly with your relatively high-wage economy in Chinese terms.

MASAHIRO KAWAI: I don't think the Japanese industry is very worried about low-wage competitiveness coming from China. They are producing very different kinds of products, and during the 1980s, Japan established an international division of labor across Asia and the Pacific Ocean by pushing out our inefficient factories and industries. It's a nice division of labor from the viewpoint of Japanese manufacturers. In the very long run, however, since the size of China's population is more than one billion people, or ten times as much as the Japanese, once their per capita income rises—and it's rising very fast now—the economic scale will be quite comparable to that of Japan or could even exceed it, and that's causing some alarm from a political and military perspective. But not in the next ten years. Low-wage competition? I don't think that's really an issue.

I just want to add one word about the Clinton administration's focus on education, competition, and investment. I think it's true that the Japanese government wanted George Bush to be reelected, because the Japanese government and business wanted to see freer trade continue. They feared that the Clinton administration would be quite protectionist. At the same time, however, the Japanese government and businesses were saying during the Bush administration that the United States should become stronger, should invest more, should increase productivity and so forth, and now we are seeing some activity along those lines.

A strong United States is quite preferable from the viewpoint of Japan. Japan doesn't want to be a leader. Japan wants somehow always to be number two, and Japan wants to have a big brother. That's really the mentality. So when the Japanese economy grows and threatens areas of the U.S. economy, the truth is that the Japanese government and businesses don't know what to do. That's really where they're coming from.

MASAHIRO YODA: Actually in comparing the labor markets in Japan and the U.S., in Japan we don't have new immigrants or new laborers from overseas countries, and in this country, of course, you always have a supply of new labor. Also, they are educated. You still have the best kind of labor force. For Japan in the short term, as Merton

Miller mentioned, there is concern about the pressure of cheaper labor from Asian countries to some extent; but in the long term Japan's practical intention is to establish international divisions of labor. So Japanese industries will be moving overseas for cheaper labor.

Not only are they looking for cheaper wages, but also, like Honda or Toyota, Japanese industries are moving out in consideration of trade frictions. In the long term I'm rather concerned about the de-industrialization of Japanese industry. In this country productivity is still very high, but most industries are moving their factories overseas. If Americans would try to produce some very good products in their own country it would help the improvement of its balance of payments.

Questions and Answers

QUESTION: I'd like to ask Professor Tobin to comment on a few points that I think are interrelated. It seems there is a lot of debate within the Clinton administration about whether to have an industrial policy or not. What are your views on this? I also wondered if you could say something about Robert Eisner's view of the budget deficit. (He says there is no deficit.) Lastly, what role should government take in increasing productivity? I wonder whether the low rise in productivity in the United States in recent years has been due to the fact that so much of our research and development has been in the military rather than the civilian sector.

JAMES TOBIN: On industrial policy, I don't think that this administration is going to be in the business of picking winners in the private sector to subsidize on any big scale. I think their main emphasis is going to be on doing the things that governments can and should do, and doing more of them and doing them better, or helping the state and local governments do more of them and do them better.

Some things like transportation, the high-speed rail, and so on, probably need government to take a leadership role. It remains to be seen whether they're worth it, or at least what should be spent on them. I do think the main emphasis is going to be on more R&D both by government and the private sector, converting DARPA (Defense Advanced Research Projects Agency) from the Pentagon into civilian research and development, assistance to the economy, and improving education, a very hard thing to accomplish.

As for productivity increasing, what can the government do? Aside from those direct programs that involve public investment, in the long run I don't think it does any good. In 1993 deficit reduction is a way of increasing national saving and full employment, increasing the amount of investment. Slowly, gradually, almost imperceptibly that will increase productivity in the future.

That's the point of deficit reduction. It's not a goal for its own sake. The whole purpose of deficit reduction is to do better for future generations: If the things you do to reduce the deficit in a slack economy, a weak economy, result in less investment rather than more, actually weakening the economy further in the process, that purpose is defeated. So do it at a time when the additional saving by the government, or the least dissaving of the government, will actually bear fruit in higher investment rather than being wasted in higher unemployment.

Robert Eisner would agree with that, so in that sense I agree with him. What I don't agree with is that there is no deficit. To put it more exactly, by any definition of deficit, whether you use Eisner's or the conventional ones, the deficit has definitely grown much larger since 1980. It has reduced national saving, and the level of the deficit and of the national saving has been underestimated every year by using conventional measures rather than Eisner's measures.

RICHARD ZECKHAUSER: I think probably Eisner was worried about undue alarm about the deficit in the late 1970s, and then he carried that over, critically, to a time when there was really a legitimate reason for being worried about the increase in the deficit.

QUESTION: Professor Zeckhauser, you were talking about the potential for investment in Japan in the next decade. What about the fact that Japan itself is investing overseas in Southeast Asia, and according to some sources is going to be the economic superpower of the twenty-first century? Also you were talking about R&D. In Japan R&D is generally sponsored by the government, and I think we're tardy in realizing that government investment is an important step for improving education, production, and industry in general. Semitec in Austin, Texas is trying to do something about R&D, but we're just beginning. We're in the initial stages compared to other countries. Also, you talked about Microsoft. I was wondering if you knew that Bill Gates, the founder, dropped out of Harvard at 19. Not to use him as an example, but, you know, sometimes facts and perspectives have a way of reversing themselves in illuminating ways.

RICHARD ZECKHAUSER: First of all, I agree that Japan is investing a lot more than we are. What I'm worried about is our investing somewhat more in Japan. I think if the U.S. did invest more in Japan, it would be a signal that we're doing better. We would end up exporting more, and we would also end up understanding the Japanese economic system better. You have to have a presence on the ground in order to be part of the economic fabric of a nation. I didn't know Bill Gates dropped out of Harvard. The people who should be most concerned about Bill Gates dropping out of Harvard are the fundraisers there, who are about to launch a $1 million drive. He could provide the full amount all by himself, which would be a very nice gesture.

I think that the Semitec investment is unclear at best. That's probably not the way the United States does its R&D best. I would prefer to see investment tax credits or equivalent sorts of level playing field types of measures as opposed to having government going into collaborative efforts. I have heard Semitec mentioned 600 times in the last two years. In its day, I used to hear about the Manhattan Project. I don't think the Manhattan Project was very successful, certainly not ecologically, for reasons that had nothing to do with the degree of investment. I don't think that we can compare ourselves in this instance with Japan. Japan is a totally different society, and what works well there is not necessarily going to work well in the United States. So Semitec is ambiguous here.

We do have lots of successes to learn from, however, and I would like to try and find out what it is that causes an Intel or a Microsoft to be successful, unbelievably successful by any standards you could conceivably ascribe to any government sorts of research activity. The answer then is that I don't want to learn much from abroad about government subsidies in R&D. I do want to learn from abroad about the important stuff, and I think that fortunately the Clinton administration is interested in doing that as well. To the extent that they start going in the directions that Professor Tobin mentioned, well, maybe we should do the calculations and figure out whether a high-speed rail would work. I'm a little bit suspicious there, however, because I think it's very hard for government to do honest calculations on itself.

MERTON MILLER: I just want to help you with the vocabulary a little. When Europe builds Airbus, that's a subsidy. But when we do it, it's a government industry branch.

QUESTION: I was wondering if any of the panelists would care to comment on the need for new economic indices in measuring economic health, and the best ways of moving forward. I have a little difficulty with gross domestic product, because I think it measures more gross consumption than it does productivity and efficiency and quality necessarily. I think if I went out and bought a solar water heater and it worked pretty well tomorrow, gross domestic consumption or gross domestic product would peak, and then next year it would drop off because I wasn't using as much gas. So in those kinds of areas do you see a need for new economic indicators?

JAMES TOBIN: It's probably not possible to have a single indicator that will serve for all the purposes that you might want to use it. Gross domestic product or gross national product is a good measure of production in the economy. Over time it goes up and down, and this means something. You can see what it means. But that doesn't mean over long periods of time that our welfare has increased by the same amount. As an indicator, GDP omits some things like leisure time or police services or the building of prisons, which might better reflect an increasing quality of life. Then we have the question of estimating environmental damage versus improvements in the environment. This is another problem.

As a person who made a modest effort to produce a modification of GNP that could be used more as a welfare indicator, I don't really think that you can just substitute one sector indicator for another. We've had lots of different indicators of economic and social health in our society, and we have to put up with the fact that we need a vector and not a single scanner number.

QUESTION: I want to ask Professor Zeckhauser about the emerging new organizations that you talked about, specifically horizontal firms versus vertically integrated firms. Are there any other points you want to elaborate on?

RICHARD ZECKHAUSER: I don't think so. What I'm trying to suggest is that academics tend to develop optimal prescriptions for things that are five years old. Governments develop them for things that are ten years old. I wanted to start thinking of the future and speculating on the idea that probably we're going to need to have more products that put components together to make a composite package, not to get something like a 586 chip coming out of a company like Apple Computer. If you think, as I do, that in the future there are going to be significant technological advances, maybe you'll think in terms of whether we could be better equipped to utilize those advances. At the present time the major U.S. firms are ill equipped, and maybe some of the Japanese giants aren't structured enough either in relation to the new technologies. It's all speculation.

QUESTION: In an article in the *Economist* in January I indicated that although the U.S.'s spending on R&D is not as high as Japan's, our implementation of R&D is more effective. I was wondering if the panelists could comment on that perspective in terms of the Clinton administration and also the APEC formation that Professor Kawai had mentioned. In other words, how are the U.S. and Japan working not only simultaneously or with each other but also with those other entities and with APEC as an economic corporation?

MASAHIRO KAWAI: APEC is a regional corporation where some institutional differences are equalized. It is basically a hodgepodge of different interests that are agreeing to a kind of loose economic cooperation. But it's not a free trade area or an institution that tries to establish a single decision maker, like to some extent the EU or NAFTA. I don't think it's going to have a really big effect on productivity, or on the effective implementation of R&D in either Japan or the United States.

CHAPTER 8

Recent Economic Trends and Japan-U.S. Relations under the Clinton Administration

March 8, 1994

MERTON MILLER

I was amused when I saw the latest issue of *Japan and the World Economy*. There's a lovely article by K. Miyagawa in which he refers to the Japanese distribution system, and notes that even if by chance they actually overturned that Japanese retailing law about which there's been so much complaint, it is by no means clear that that would have any effect on increasing Japanese imports. That whole line of guff has been grossly oversold. I didn't think these quotas would have any serious effect on anything, but they didn't have any great cost either. They were just so much talk.

All that changes, however, the minute you start talking about bringing Super 301 (the clause introduced by the Bush administration to force Japan to open its market to American goods) back out of the closet and start talking seriously about trade retaliation. That way I think lies disaster, not just for American and Japanese consumers but for the whole world. I can only hope that there's still time for the administration to come to its senses and to back off from this crazy game of chicken that it's playing with Japan.

Frankly I'm not terribly hopeful, because having reaped so much political benefit from demonizing Japan I think Clinton now has to make good on his tough talk or he has another Bosnia on his hands. So I'm fairly pessimistic about that. As an economist I have to believe a Pareto-improving solution will always emerge, but I'm worried about it.

I'm worried about one other thing, and I will close on that note. I think that the administration's pushing so hard on the export line is actually going to strengthen the hands of the MOF bureaucrats and the MITI bureaucrats that I detest so much, and that I think are a very negative part of Japanese economic life. They can say now:

> Look. All this pious talk from the Americans about free trade and so on, it's clear now as we told you all along that that doesn't really mean anything. They know and we know that trade is just another form of warfare. We try to penetrate their markets, they try to penetrate our markets. At the moment we happen to be a little down and at a disadvantage, but we're all playing the same sort of mercantilist game.

I think Clinton's hard line is going to strengthen their hands against the reformist wing of politicians that I see finally starting to spring up in Japan, which would be a shame. I will say no more for now, but we can discuss these issues further during the Panel Discussion.

I turn it over to Jim.

JAMES TOBIN

Merton Miller and I have appeared on a number of platforms together and we always disagree, so it's unfortunate in a way that I have to agree with most of what he said this morning on this topic. Actually I wrote a piece in the *Boston Globe* about this the other day. I'm not going to read it but I'm going to draw upon it brazenly in my remarks this morning, as I assume not very many people here read the *Boston Globe.*

Perhaps people have forgotten that it was only last July that Clinton was in Tokyo for the G-7 meeting where he and the Japanese Prime Minister adopted the so-called framework for a New Economic Partnership between Japan and the United States, amid a good deal of fanfare. I went to the trouble of reading that document just the other day, and it's actually quite moderate. It does not say that there's a sinfulness in bilateral imbalances of trade, and it doesn't suggest that there should be any numerical targets for the bilateral balance or for the overall Japanese surplus, although it does refer to the surplus—the overall surplus, not the bilateral one—as a problem. The closest it comes to talking about targets and quotas is to endorse objective criteria for progress in the various trade relations to be negotiated in the framework agreement.

It does say that the criteria could be both qualitative and quantitative, but the main idea was that there would be meetings, continuous meetings, on all kinds of joint problems between the two countries, including AIDS and a lot of other nontrade issues. Each subject would be monitored in frequent meetings of bilateral committees, and there would be a biannual summit meeting between the President and the Prime Minister about these matters.

This all seemed set to go last year. It was very different in tone from the acrimony we had the other day when the Summit broke up in Washington, eight months later. The framework agreement had no chance to work. It was adopted only last July, before Hosokawa was Prime Minister. This fit of anger, this breaking off of further negotiations, was not only early in the tenure of Hosokawa but also early in the lifetime, the supposed lifetime, of the framework agreement. Clearly there was a lot of accumulated bitterness and resentment toward Japanese trade and the Japanese economy behind what happened last month, feelings that did not have anything to do with the validity of the framework agreement itself.

Now a lot of things didn't happen as we might have hoped. The macroeconomic measures last summer that were supposed to pep up the Japanese economy and in the process pep up Japanese demand for foreign goods, including American goods, didn't work out that way. Actually recession in Japan got worse, and the recovery measures that the government tried to get through were not only fairly mild as such measures go but they didn't even get through the Diet. The bilateral imbalance, not even mentioned in the framework agreement, got worse, and so did the overall Japanese surplus.

I think it's still true that the best vehicle for restoring relationships right now and for cooling off the trade war would be just to return to the framework agreement. It's not the document that Merton Miller and I would have written, but it's a reasonable document for getting back on track. I think it could be phrased in a way to give both the Clinton administration and the Japanese a face-saving way out of the current impasse.

Bill Clinton obviously likes playing a very active role in international trade policy. In fact I think at times he has tended to equate international economics with foreign policy. How he wishes that were true! I mean it's easier than Bosnia, Somalia, or Russia, and all those other problems that keep intruding upon his time and attention.

Also, he has reason to be worried about the fragility of the recovery, which has gone on pretty well during his first year in office. He was not able to put any fiscal policy for recovery into his program. He was forced to devote the entire budget to reducing the budget deficit, rather than to his own public investment program or toward giving the economy a boost. Then the Federal Reserve, which was seemingly cooperative with the Clinton recovery until February 4, all of a sudden saw an inflation that nobody else could see and raised the Federal funds rate target by 25 basis points, setting off a very puzzling response in the financial markets. Greenspan intimated that his taking this action on the short-term rate would actually cause long-term rates to fall, because it would be such a reassurance to the market that the Federal Reserve hadn't gone to sleep about the possible danger of inflation.

Well, instead of causing long-term rates to fall, it caused them to rise by more than the increase in the short-term rate. That probably won't last, but certainly Greenspan threw the financial markets for a loop, such a loop that George Soros apparently acted like a rational economist in believing that the trade war prospects would cause the dollar to appreciate—and instead of that the dollar depreciated and the yen appreciated, thus losing him $600 million. (Only a small part of the amount he had gained on the British pound a couple of years earlier, so I wouldn't feel too sorry for him.)

At any rate, Clinton's enthusiasm for doing trade policy in an active way was shown by his making the NAFTA and the GATT-Uruguay Round his own crusades, even though they had been started actually by previous administrations. All the time he keeps saying that exports, exports, exports, are going to be jobs, jobs, jobs, and I think he does see exports as the main source of job creation, given the fragility of the recovery and the absence of domestic fiscal and monetary stimulus.

But Clinton seems to be schizophrenic on trade policy. On the one hand he was for NAFTA and the Uruguay Round and GATT, and he does have some economists in his entourage whose instincts (if not as strong as Merton Miller's), are for free trade or in that direction, people who are internationalists in economic policy. On the other hand, he also has some lawyers who apparently were frustrated along with their clients who couldn't make their desired arrangements in Japan, and who have accumulated grievances in addition from their private life. So we have on the one hand a part of the team that is internationalist and multilateral in its approach, and on the other hand a group of hard-line protectionists. Clinton has sometimes been on one side and sometimes on the other.

We know as economists that America does not come into these arguments about who's interfering with trade with clean hands or with any license for self-righteous complaints about the sins of the rest of the world, whether the European Community or Japan. As a matter of fact the rest of the world knows very well about America's own restrictions on imports, all our quotas and retaliations. According to the *Financial Times,* they have no sympathy with the United States in this quarrel with Japan.

The internationalist view, which one would have hoped the Clinton administration would stick with, is that we are for multilateral trade, we're for rules of the game that are agreed throughout the world. We're not for free trade, that's impossible, but at least we have rules of the game and we have neutral internationalist arbitrations of trade disputes in the GATT. Japan picks up a lot of points in the world community by saying they're willing to do that while the United States tries to be bilateral, appointing itself prosecutor, judge, and jury on Japan's alleged infringements.

I think Prime Minister Hosokawa is quite justified in resisting the idea of agreed numerical targets for shares of American or other imports in particular industries, auto parts, semiconductors, or whatnot. Japan had a bad experience with the semiconductor agreement. They mentioned a figure, intending it to be a kind of approximate, desirable goal. Then, when it didn't quite materialize, the United States acted as if it were a contract that had been breached. It's pretty understandable that Hosokawa doesn't want to agree on any more specific numerical results.

It is ironic that just when they have a politician, a Prime Minister, who is probably more than the previous ones dedicated to deregulating the Japanese market, not just deregulating it from official restraints of trade but from the unofficial coziness of Japanese relationships among themselves, that we all of a sudden say we've had enough of this and it's got to stop.

What we're really asking in many cases is not the lifting of official barriers, which are very rare—there are no tariffs, but there are certain official discriminations against foreign suppliers that we have good reason to oppose and ask to have corrected—but in large degree we are essentially saying that what we want is for the Japanese to arrange to purchase more of our stuff, and to change their tastes and their habits. Obviously that's not something we ourselves would be prepared to do. If anybody said, "We want a certain share of right-hand steering wheel cars to be purchased in America," we would laugh them out of court.

The most important thing Japan could do right now is I think quite consistent with the relations that the major macroeconomic powers of the world have with each other—namely to have some coordination of macroeconomic policies in the interest of the world as a whole. In this case Japan's part would be to take vigorous measures of macroeconomic fiscal stimulus—government spending for their own public investment purposes, tax reduction to get them out of the recession—that would have a by-product of increased demand by the Japanese for imports from everywhere, including the United States.

It would be better to achieve that recovery in Japanese domestic policy by a fiscal stimulus than by monetary easing. Monetary easing would tend to depreciate the yen, and as far as the surplus and the balance of trade are concerned, that would set things back compared with a domestic fiscal policy that would provide the stimulus itself. I think it's certainly within general internationally acceptable behavior for the United States and the other G-7 countries to continue pressure on Japan to take that kind of macro measure. After all, the current account surplus of Japan is largely a macroeconomic phenomenon. It reflects the excess of Japanese domestic saving over its own domestic investment, and the opposite tendency in the United States. We are not going to solve the imbalances of current accounts of trade unless we solve those macroeconomic discrepancies. Doing little things with this specific industry and that specific industry just shifts those imbalances around and does not get rid of them.

I'm happy to be surrounded by distinguished scholars rather than the malcontent, frustrated lawyers of the Clinton administration. I'd like to comment on the current U.S.-Japan trade issue.

Just after the inauguration last year it became clear that the new Clinton administration's strategy toward Japan placed an emphasis on quantitative results in trade negotiations. During the first year of the administration there was an expectation that the Japanese-American relationship would move in a new and positive direction, especially with the added incentive of a new government in Japan led by Prime Minster Hosokawa, which promised change.

Unfortunately, this expectation of change in a positive direction between our two countries has yet to be realized. Instead, the U.S.-Japan relationship has come to a point resembling a worst-case scenario. In fact, we could probably say that we have reached an impasse on the improvement of relations, since the U.S.-Japan Summit failed to produce a new trade policy when it concluded in Washington on February 11.

This failed Summit resulted in the unexpected strengthening of the Japanese yen, which might further weaken the struggling Japanese economy. To prevent the further strengthening of the yen, Japan could open its market to imports. At the same time the Clinton administration has revived the Super 301 clause to force Japan to open its market to American goods, and there is renewed interest by the U.S. Congress to impose retaliatory trade sanctions against Japanese imports. The whole situation gives the appearance of a trade war.

As someone doing business here in the United States I have serious concerns about the present situation and additional apprehension about how we can solve these serious problems. It appears that both our governments have unusual expectations, and a reality gap exists between them that very likely has contributed to the breakdown of the recent trade talks in Washington.

The Japanese may have overestimated the level of trust and confidence that President Clinton had in Prime Minister Hosokawa. They did not give enough consideration to the powerful effect their saying no would have on the negotiations. On the other hand, the Americans believed that if they showed a strong stance on trade, such a position would without fail lead to compromise from the Japanese. In addition, the Americans may have overestimated Morihiro Hosokawa's ability to deal effectively with the Japanese bureaucracy.

The two main themes of the trade talks between Japan and the United States were trade surplus reduction by the Japanese government through macroeconomic policy and the establishment of measures to open specific market sectors such as automobiles and the financial markets. The Japanese objected to establishing new American targets on either macro or micro levels, which led directly to the collapse of the discussion last month.

I strongly feel that there is a perception gap on several points when it comes to the U.S.-Japan trade imbalance. The trade imbalance shows a huge surplus for Japan, this is for sure, and the assumption is that this is because Japan's markets are closed and Japan imports very little. Let me begin by saying that the growth of Japan's surplus has finally begun to slow down. Japan's trade surplus with the United States appears to have peaked in the middle of 1993, and the economic slowdown in Japan has put a damper on any increase in imports.

Japan's current export growth rate compared with last year became negative. It is expected that economic recovery in Japan will be accompanied by a gradual increase in imports as the surplus continues to show a decreasing trend. As far as the figures for the U.S.-Japan imbalance, looking at them from the American viewpoint the deficit with Japan increased to over $59 billion in 1993, a sharp rise from $41 billion in 1990. That figure accounts for 50 percent of the total American trade deficit. This deficit increased because the U.S. increased imports from Japan while its exports to Japan remained the same or shrank due to the recession in Japan.

Japanese exports to the United States in particular increased 10.4 percent in 1993 compared with 1992. This rise in imports from Japan was a result of the recovery of the American economy. As a consequence there was a sharp increase in demand for machinery and equipment—

fax machines and copiers as well as semiconductors. Japan supplies virtually all the world's fax machines, copiers, and LCDs. Japan and America cooperate to produce computers. The Japanese make memory chips, while the Americans make the CPUs.

Many Americans believe that Japan is a country that imports very little, but next to Canada Japan is in fact America's largest trading partner. Last year Japan imported $48 billion of American goods, roughly 10 percent of America's total exports of $465 billion. Venezuela and Mexico follow Japan as America's third and fourth largest trading partners. Total American exports to Japan are even larger than the total amount to Great Britain and Germany combined. Total American exports to Japan are even larger than the total of American exports to all of South America.

Rice was a topic of discussion last year. The fact is that Japan is the largest export market for America's agricultural products, totalling $7.7 billion in 1991. The export total to the entire European Union for the same period was $6.9 billion. So much for the belief that Japan imports very little. When we look at the trade facts in this way we see a great change, and we also see the character of the U.S.-Japan trade relationship as one of increased interdependence and a competition which is wholesome and healthy in the long term.

The trade imbalance of $59 billion, the number that grabs our immediate attention, reflects the nature of each country's trade structure and perhaps it is the difference in economic conditions between our two countries at the present time that makes Japan's surplus seem larger than it actually is. I can appreciate the criticism that Japanese response to the trade imbalance has been delayed in coming, but on the other hand it can also be said that the managed trade concept the Clinton administration is attempting to promote is counterproductive and even dangerous in a world economy that is becoming increasingly interdependent.

Let me say a few words about the Japanese economy. Some indicators seem to suggest that the Japanese economy has bottomed out, and from here we should expect an economic loss of about 0.5 percent in 1994. However, there's the present exchange rate. Actually this gross rate is calculated and the yen-dollar rate is now 113 yen. If the present exchange rate were to continue at about the 105 level, there is a concern that all the positive indicators would disappear and that Japan might experience a two-year period of negative economic growth unprecedented in the last fifty years, since the end of World War II.

If the Japanese economy continues to be weak, there is a concern that rather than seeing an increase of imports we will witness a cycle of even larger trade surplus. In America indicators seem to suggest that the economy is finally gathering momentum after three years of being slow and weak. A weak dollar may give further rise to inflation, and there would be impetus for a rising interest rate. With that would come a fear of the destabilization of financial markets. The continuation of trade talks is essential to calm everybody's fears.

Just as the United States established a target to reduce its international debt by $500 billion over the next five years, it is my opinion that Japan had better set a nominal goal for its trade surplus to be about 2 percent of its GDP. It is absolutely essential for Japan to take immediate measures through fiscal policy stimulation to mobilize its economy, now stuck in the middle of the worst recession in its history. Establishing numerical targets in specific areas, however, distorts the normal supply and demand relationship. Since doing that places unnecessary constraint on Japanese consumers, I feel Japan should certainly be opposed to such numerical targets.

If America sets such targets it won't be long before other countries do the same. It is a strong concern that managed trade will change the direction of free trade. One might ask why President Clinton would adhere to this managed trade policy. To avoid managed trade Prime Minister Hosokawa must propose an alternative, the relaxation of regulatory constraints on imports that prevent Japanese consumers from getting cheaper and better goods from other countries, and he must make a concentrated effort to ensure that both domestic and foreign companies doing business in Japan have a level playing field of competition in the Japanese market.

Japan is a culture that has unique customs and treats non-Japanese in a manner that is often indirect and lacking in clarity. I think it is essential for Japan to decide specifically what it wants to preserve and what it is willing to change regarding its cultural and business customs. Before we take up the discussion of numbers to settle the trade dispute, we need to decide what direction our trade relations should take.

It is my opinion that the time has come for our two governments to conduct among our best economists serious, level-headed discussions, such as the type we are engaged in here today. Economists and representatives of the business community must work together to create the framework for resolving the trade imbalance between our two countries.

RICHARD ZECKHAUSER

I'd like to talk about three dialogues this morning: First is the dialogue that has taken place over the past ten or fifteen years, principally among economists; second is an internal dialogue in the United States about how we should think about foreign trade and what it does to our country; and third is the dialogue between the United States and Japan.

I've been looking at these issues for the past fifteen years, and every year that we've had the symposium here or that I've spoken in Japan the term "trade war" has come up. While we often haven't had perfect trading relations, we've been so far from a trade war that I think the "good news" is a bit like the good news during the cold war: Everybody always said we were perched on the edge of nuclear annihilation, and yet we always managed to stay very far away from it. That doesn't mean that we shouldn't be cautious, but we shouldn't assume we're always just on the verge of a trade war.

The most interesting thing about the first dialogue is that it goes on no matter what the conditions are. When I first started going to Japan, the United States was doing pretty well. In the 1980s the Japanese economy was in fact doing much better than we were, however, and the economic reputation of the United States was severely oversold. As a consequence, Japan had a dramatically exaggerated view of our capabilities. Now the tables have been turned, but the discussion is (usually) the same. So it doesn't matter what the economic conditions are in the United States. As long as Japan runs a trade surplus, it will be blamed for conditions in this country. I disagree with that view.

As an aside, I should tell you there's very good news for the United States. From 1991 to 1992 productivity in the United States was up over 4 percent. In Japan, by contrast, it declined by more than 5 percent. The United States was the largest exporter in the world for the first time since 1980. We account for 13 percent of the world's merchandise exports. Jobs are increasing nicely in the United States. Everybody assumes that Japan is the chip maker to the world, but for the first time since 1988, in 1991–92 the United States was the largest manufacturer of semiconductor chips. These things are all happening, yet our trade deficit with Japan stays strongly unfavorable or favorable—however you might like to talk about it.

Let me turn next to the dialogue in the United States about trade. With the NAFTA debate, the terms "prices" and "costs" were not mentioned. You weren't allowed to say that things would be cheaper for the typical American, or even the typical poor American, because NAFTA was about jobs, with the environment as a slight subtext. Now that's very interesting in light of Professor Miller's comments about the importance of serving consumers, that one of the big advantages of our extraordinarily open economy is that we can buy things about as cheaply as you can anywhere in the world. It's important at least to mention that part of the original motivation for free trade was enabling people to get more consumer goods for the same amount of resources. Why more attention is not paid to the consumer benefits from free trade is a puzzle.

A second puzzle is the relationship between trade and the differential in wages between skilled and unskilled labor in the United States. A severe problem in America now is that the gap between wages for skilled and un-skilled workers has increased dramatically. The explanation is rather straightforward; we are importing low-wage goods from overseas, and that's making our lower-wage producers try to compete. They do this by paying very low wages. The only trouble with this explanation, which could in theory be true, is that it's not true. In fact, on a value-added basis our average trading partner has a wage that's 88 percent of ours, very high relative to our wages.

The ratio of skilled to unskilled labor has been increasing. This suggests that the principal factor driving this growing wage differential, which I think is going to be a major policy problem in the United States for years to come, is not trade, but developments in our own domestic economy. Paul Krugman and Robert Lawrence estimated that at most 10 percent of our increasing wage differential should be attributed to trade. Now trade is a wonderful bogeyman; it is intangible, so it's always very attractive to blame all of our problems on it.

The third dialogue I'd like to talk about is the one we're having with Japan. I think the United States is largely putting the dialogue in the hands of the wrong people, and we may be focusing only on one issue—not the one economists like to talk about. I find it ironic. I wish that we had more economists in the administration. I find it disturbing that a lobbyist who happens to be a lawyer is in charge of our trade policy, because I think that a legal-lobbying background dramatically affects an official's outlook.

I can identify four areas where we could try to work out arrangements with Japan if we were upset about the deficit. The first is the area of tariffs and quotas, and I think that's a real loser. It's a loser economically; I think it's also a loser politically. The United States, which has been the principal nation supporting international economic arrangements in the postwar era, can't and won't be seen as the principal country that violates some of these arrangements, and I think that Super 301 is so powerful that it's really hard to use it in any significant way. We bring the sword out of the sheath and we leave it lying on a table for a period of time, and then for months and months and months everybody tries to back away from it. I predict that we won't use it to any significant extent.

The second area, which was mentioned by Professor Tobin, is domestic policy. Now we always have wonderful ideas about the domestic policies that other countries should adopt. This past spring we had a little discussion ourselves about what our domestic policies should have been, and wonder how we would have felt if Prime Minister Hosokawa or some French or German figure had "weighed in" as to whether the United States should have really had a significant or modest or no stimulus whatsoever. I think that we would have rightly said, "That's our business, and we don't want you to tell us what to do."

We could have multilateral negotiations on coordinating macroeconomic policy, but I think it's unrealistic for any country to expect that another country is going to dramatically shift its domestic policies to help us out. Maybe there will be a fortunate confluence of interests. If Professor Tobin were advising Japan he would give them advice that would turn out to be good for American exporters, and that's great. But I don't think we should be so naive as to expect that to play a significant role.

The third area, already mentioned much by economists but likely to become increasingly important to everyone, is military policy. People talk about the foreign affairs world being in somewhat of a shambles. We are in a new, multipolar world where nobody understands what is going to happen, and the United States is in a much more secure position than Japan. Japan has to worry about Korea, a sort of small outlaw country that may or may not have nuclear weapons and may or may not want to use them. Succession there is very unclear. As you remember, we were scared to death when Cuba got a few nuclear-tipped missiles. How would you feel if you were sitting in Japan today, with the United States protecting you? China is nearby, and nobody knows what China is going to do. Let's hope China continues on its present course of very rapid economic growth and ends up being a great trading partner for both the United States and Japan—but this outcome is uncertain.

I think this last is an area where there will be some discussion. I strongly hope that the United States does not try to exert significant leverage on Japan in military affairs. I wouldn't mind if Japan paid an extra $10 billion toward the common defense, which they would pay toward us, but I don't think that we want to force Japan to be more on its own militarily or dramatically any more than it would be otherwise. Many Japanese and many Americans would not like to see that happen, but I think the possibility is sitting there in the background.

In the fourth area I'm a little pessimistic. Pressure is building in the United States over the long run to do something about the trade imbalance. The United States will start to discover that all of its other tools are inappropriate or infeasible, and will probably do some things that don't violate GATT but which will come closer to a strategic trade policy than we have been in the past. Examples are giving preference to American companies in bidding on construction projects, or limiting the numbers of Japanese students who study at American universities. I predict that not in the next year but over the next five or ten years we'll see more instruments like this, because everybody says, "Japan has all those things that they can do and we don't have anything we can do," and then people say, "Well, what can we do?" There is infinite creativity in Washington, not always well directed.

I like to talk about the U.S. and Japan in an Olympics

metaphor. Sometimes I've talked about bicycle racing and how easy it is to be in the competitor's stream. The most interesting Olympic event I saw this year, which I hope does not describe our relationship, was the short-track speed skating. The skaters elbow each other in the turns, and frequently two or three people go down at the same time. I think that's a poor metaphor for what's happening with the United States and Japan. I'd like to think of us more as being in something like a 1,000 kilometer ski race: Each can help the other establish world records, and there are no Tonya Hardings involved. I'd like to think that Japan and the United States in the postwar world both deserve gold medals, not unlike Oksana Baiul and Nancy Kerrigan.

PANEL DISCUSSION

MERTON MILLER: I agree with Richard Zeckhauser about the issue of fiscal stimulus, but I'd add that it's by no means clear that it would work as neatly as Jim Tobin thinks it would. It works on the blackboard, but it's by no means clear that it would work in practice. I also accept Richard's point that we can't persuade our own people to engage in the kind of fiscal stimulus that Jim would like to see, because the American people may not think the proposed government projects are worth the money. I don't see why anyone should be surprised that the Japanese feel the same way. So I put much less weight on that than Jim does.

I'm more worried than Richard is about retaliation. There are people in the Clinton administration who want the negotiations to fail so that they can adopt a thoroughly restrictionist policy. I don't know how powerful they are in the administration, because nobody really knows at the moment who's in power in the administration—but those people really worry me.

JAMES TOBIN: The consultation among the G-7 countries about macroeconomic policy has been going on for a long time, and almost invariably in the last ten years the G-7 communiqué has said that the various governments at the Summit there advise or hope or urge that the United

States take strong measures to reduce its deficit. That has been an invariable recommendation by Japan and the other five countries besides the United States, and each time our government has said, "Why, sure. That's what we want to do, too." This is the first time we've actually done something, but the other countries have suggested again and again what our principal policy should be, for a long, long time.

Japan itself agreed at the Summit that they need an expansionary fiscal policy. It's not an external thing being imposed upon them, but it has seemed that when the government actually goes back to Tokyo and proposes it then somehow it doesn't get done by the Parliament. I think it's true that none of the things that we're talking about here are going to all of a sudden eliminate the Japanese current account surplus. Whether they're macro or micro they're not going to do that. But at least the macro ones are going in the right direction, both for the world as a whole and for Japan itself. It's not we who say Japan needs more infrastructure. That's their own idea, and fiscal stimulus can of course be given either on the spending side of the budget or on the tax reduction side of the budget.

RICHARD ZECKHAUSER: Super 301 was invoked by the United States once before. That was during the Bush administration, not the Clinton administration. They actually went through with it, and found some particular cases where they were going to impose sanctions on Japan if Japan didn't shape up. We aimed at India and Brazil at the same time. In none of these cases, however, did we actually do anything in the end.

MASAHIRO YODA: As far as the government stimulus package in Japan is concerned, they are going to prepare 15 trillion yen out of pocket. Tax deduction, mostly income tax deduction, is over 5 trillion yen, and it's going to be effective. In the beginning the Hosokawa administration was planning to have a multiyear, two- or three-year tax deduction before they introduced the welfare tax. They were trying to increase the purchase tax, the tax on consumption. Suddenly they changed the name to the welfare tax, and they withdrew overnight. Unfortunately the plan didn't work out, but they had the intention to reduce income tax for three years, although the government officials couldn't say anything when they came to Washington and even Tsutomu Hata, the Minister of Foreign Affairs, couldn't promise that it was going to be three years or multiyears. I think out of $15 trillion yen maybe two-thirds would work out as a stimulus. Tax cuts and government expenditures on investment will work, but the part of the package that would simply replace expenditures by the private sector is not going to help.

As for the exchange rate, everybody is mentioning 105 yen. At one time they said it would be impossible for Japanese industries to adjust to 110 yen, but now I think they are maybe 75 or 80 percent there. Still, it takes time. As far as three-year growth is concerned, I think there is a great possibility that the Japanese economy won't grow at all if the exchange rate continues at this level.

RICHARD ZECKHAUSER: This discussion makes me think of Japan and the U.S. as a squabbling couple. Somebody points out, "They just threw some china; they broke the dishes. This is pretty serious!" The questions are: "Have you ever spent a night apart?" "Has he ever punched anybody in anger?" And the answer to both of those questions is really no. I think that's actually a fairly hopeful lesson, because what it means is that both sides are so scared of what could happen that they won't let it happen. The questions now are: "How can we create a meaningful dialogue within that context?" and "What role can the people in this room play in making that dialogue more fruitful and productive?"

MARTI SUBRAHMANYAM: I hope you're right, Richard, but I don't know. Nobody in the rest of the world likes to be lectured to constantly by the United States government. Nobody likes to be told constantly how to run their economy.

As you pointed out, we don't like people to tell us how to run our economy, either. I remember a couple of years ago the Japanese government submitted a list of 150 things that the U.S. should do to reform its society, including how to run our urban police departments. Would we like to accept this kind of list constantly about micro managing our society and economy? I think the same thing is true whether you lecture India about opening up its insurance business or Brazil about how to run its orange juice business or Japan about importing more rice.

There are cultural barriers to overcome. Although I

cannot share Merton Miller's pessimism that this time things may go too far, it does seem to me that talks are breaking down. I think before that happens we need to look for an intermediary who can get people to talk sense to each other.

Speaker Profiles

Editor's Note: The following profiles represent the titles of the panelists at the time of their respective lectures.

JAGDISH BHAGWATI is the Arthur Lehman Professor of Economics and Professor of Political Science at Columbia University. He is Economic Policy Advisor to the Director-General, GATT and advisor to the Finance Minister of India. He has written 200 articles and authored or edited 30 books. He writes frequently for the *New York Times*, the *Wall Street Journal*, and the *Financial Times*, reviews for the *New Republic*, and has appeared on major TV shows. He has received many honorary doctorates.

WILLEM H. BUITER is Juan T. Trippe Professor of International Economics, Yale University. He received his bachelor's degree in economics from Cambridge University in 1971 and his Ph.D. from Yale University in 1975. He was on the faculty of Princeton University, and the London School of Economics and Political Science before joining Yale University in 1985. In 1990, he was appointed as a chair professor. He has been a consultant to the Inter-American Development Bank, World Bank, and was a Visiting Scholar at the International Monetary Fund. He is the author of five books and many articles. He received the Second Annual Sanwa Monograph Award administered by the Center to write a monograph on international financial markets in 1993.

FUJIO CHO is President and CEO of Toyota Motor Manufacturing, U.S.A., Inc., in Kentucky. He joined Toyota in 1960 after graduating with a law degree from the University of Tokyo. In 1974, he became Manager of the Production Control Department, where he was instrumental in developing the company's production system. Fujio Cho was named General Manager of the Transportation Control Office in 1984 and General Manager of the North American Project Office in 1986. In 1988, he became a member of the Toyota Motor Corporation Board of Directors.

STEPHEN FIGLEWSKI is Professor of Finance and Yamaichi Faculty Fellow at the Stern School of Business. He received his B.A. from Princeton University and Ph.D. from the Massachusetts Institute of Technology. He has published extensively in the area of financial futures and options. He is editor of the *Journal of Derivatives,* and was also a senior editor and author of a recently published book, *Financial Options: From Theory to Practice.* Professor Figlewski has also worked on Wall Street as Vice President at the First Boston Corporation.

YASUSHI HAMAO is Associate Professor of Finance at the Graduate School of Business Administration at Columbia University. He received his B.A. from Columbia

University and Ph.D. from Yale University. Before joining Columbia University in 1991, he was a faculty member of the Graduate School of International Relations and Pacific Studies, University of California, and an officer of the Bank of Tokyo. A specialist on Japanese financial markets, he is the author of two books and of many articles in professional journals.

ROBERT KAVESH, moderator, is Marcus Nadler Professor of Finance and Economics at the Stern School of Business. After graduating from New York University, he received his Ph.D. from Harvard. His research interests are in economic and business forecasting techniques. He has been Executive Secretary and Treasurer of the American Finance Association (1961–79) and President of the Money Marketeers (1983–84). He received the "Great Teacher" Award of New York University in 1983.

MASAHIRO KAWAI is Associate Professor, Institute of Social Sciences, University of Tokyo and Research Scientist at the Center for Japan-U.S. Business and Economic Studies, Stern School of Business. He received his Ph.D. at Stanford University while a Research Fellow at the Brookings Institution. His fields of interest include: international finance and open macroeconomics, economics of commodity markets, and applied econometrics.

TORU KUSUKAWA is Chairman of the Fuji Research Institute Corporation. He joined the Fuji Bank after graduating from the University of Tokyo in 1950. He started his career in the International Division and (after service in Japan, England, and Germany and internships in investment banking houses in New York) was appointed as Deputy Chief Manager in the Head Office Business Division. In 1977, he was promoted as the Chief Manager of the International Division and Deputy President in 1981. In 1991, he left the bank to become Chairman of the Institute. He is also a director of Fuji-Wolfensohn International, a joint venture of Fuji Bank and James D. Wolfensohn, Incorporated.

SADAHEI KUSUMOTO is Chairman of Minolta Corporation, the American subsidiary that markets all Minolta products. In 1954, he came to the United States as the sole sales representative of Minolta. He oversaw the growth of sales from $600,000 in 1955 to $800 million today. He was named to the Photo Marketing Association Hall of Fame and in 1993 received the Foreign Minister's Award for his contribution to Japan-U.S. relations. He is the author of *My Bridge to America, Discovering the New World for Minolta*.

RICHARD LEVICH is Professor of Finance and International Business at New York University. He received his undergraduate degree, MBA, and Ph.D. from the University of Chicago. He has been a visiting faculty member at many distinguished universities in the United States and abroad. He has been a consultant or visiting scholar at the

Federal Reserve Board of Governors, the International Monetary Fund, and the World Bank. He is the author of 50 articles on various topics dealing with international finance and author or editor of nine books.

JOSHUA LIVNAT is Chairman of the Department of Accounting, Stern School of Business, New York University. He earned a B.Sc. at the Hebrew University of Jerusalem and an M.A. and Ph.D. at New York University. Among the schools where he has held visiting professorships are the University of California, Berkeley and the University of Auckland, New Zealand. He is the author of *Cash Flow and Security Analysis* (1992), as well as articles for various academic journals including the *Journal of Accounting Research*, the *Accounting Review*, and the *Journal of Accounting and Economics*.

MERTON MILLER is the Robert R. McCormick Distinguished Service Professor at the University of Chicago. He has served in the U.S. Treasury and the Board of Governors of the Federal Reserve System. He was a member of the faculty at the Carnegie Institute of Technology before moving to Chicago. His work on capital structure and dividend policy with Franco Modigliani laid the foundations of the theory of corporate finance and earned him the Nobel Prize in Economics. He is the author of many books and articles, including *Financial Innovations and Market Volatility* (1991), and is a fellow of the American Academy of the Arts and Sciences and Distinguished Fellow of the American Economic Association. Currently he is a Public Governor of the Chicago Mercantile Exchange.

SOSHICHI MIYACHI is Executive Director/Chief Commentator for Television Tokyo and Chief Commentator on the daily program "World Business Satellite." A graduate in economics from Waseda University, he worked in various positions at the Nihon Keizai Shimbun, Inc., rising to the position of Deputy Chief Editorial Writer before moving to his present position. An expert in macroeconomics and international economic policy, he is the author of nine books. In 1962, he received an award from the Japan Newspaper Publishers and Editors Association in the editorial category.

THOMAS PUGEL is Professor Economics and International Business at the Stern School. He received his Ph.D. in Economics from Harvard University in 1978. Since then he has been with NYU, and is now Chairman of the Department of International Business. He specializes in the economics of trade and investment, and in macroeconomics. In addition to numerous articles in professional journals, he is co-author of a book, *Microelectronics: An Industry in Transition* and co-editor of *Fragile Interdependence: Economic Issues in U.S.-Japanese Trade and Investment.*

PAUL A. SAMUELSON is one of the world's most notable economists. He is Long-Term Credit Bank of Japan Visiting Professor of Political Economy at the Japan-U.S. Center, New York University, as well as Institute Professor Emeritus of the Massachusetts Institute of Technology. Professor Samuelson has made definitive contributions to economics and finance. He was an adviser to Presidents Kennedy and Johnson and has been a consultant to many businesses and foundations. He is the first American recipient of the Nobel Prize in Economics, awarded in 1970, and is a regular participant in the Center's events.

RYUZO SATO is C. V. Starr Professor of Economics and Director of the Center for Japan-U.S. Business and Economic Studies. He received his bachelor's degree and Dr.Ec. from Hitotsubashi University, in addition to a Ph.D. from Johns Hopkins University. His book, *Kiku to Washi* (The Chrysanthemum and the Eagle) received the first Rondansho Award in Social Science Writing by the Yomiuri newspaper and is now available in English through NYU Press.

HIROMOTO SEKI is Consul General of Japan in New York. Ambassador Seki received his B.A. in law from the University of Tokyo and joined the diplomatic service. In his long career, he has held many responsible positions in the Ministry of Foreign Affairs in Tokyo and abroad. He was in the permanent delegation from Japan to the OECD; Director, Multinational Cooperation Division, Economic Cooperation Bureau; Director, Regional Policy

Division, Asian Affairs Bureau; and Director-General of International Affairs, Defense Agency. His foreign assignments include Thailand, the Republic of China, and the United States, where he was earlier Consul General in Los Angeles.

MARTI SUBRAHMANYAM, moderator, Sanwa series, is the Charles E. Merrill Professor of Finance and Economics at the Stern School of Business. He has been a visiting professor at leading academic institutions in England, France, Germany, and India, as well as a Visiting Chairholder at INSEAD, France and an Overseas Fellow at Churchill College, Cambridge University. He has written numerous articles and books in the areas of corporate finance, capital markets, and international finance. His latest book is *Financial Options: From Theory to Practice.*

MIKE SYNAR is the Second District Congressman of Oklahoma. He received an M.S. in management from Northwestern University before receiving a J.D. from the University of Oklahoma. With health care, energy, and economic growth as his top priorities, Congressman Synar serves on the House Committees on Energy and Commerce, Judiciary, and Government Operations. He chairs the Government Operations Subcommittee on Environment, Energy, and Natural Resources and is the Chairman of the Democratic Study Group. He was designated one of the "Cleanest Dozen" in Congress by *U.S. News and World Report* in 1989.

JAMES TOBIN, who received the Nobel Prize in Economics in 1981, is Sterling Professor Emeritus of Economics at Yale University. He has served as a consultant to various governmental agencies, including the President's Council of Economic Advisers, the Federal Reserve System, the U.S. Treasury, and the Port Authority of New York and New Jersey. In 1961–62 he was a member of President Kennedy's Council of Economic Advisers. He was awarded the John Bates Clark Medal and served as President of the American Economic Association and the Econometrics Society.

HIROSHI TSUKAMOTO is currently the President of JETRO in New York. A graduate of Kyoto University, he has served for 24 years in MITI (Japan's Ministry of International Trade and Industry) or MITI-affiliated positions. Immediately prior to this current assignment, he was Director of MITI's Policy Planning Office where he was involved in preparing Japan's long-term plan "Creating Human Values in the Global Era." He has also visited the Royal Institute of International Affairs as Visiting Scholar and Syracuse University as Overseas Senior Researcher.

MASAHIRO YODA is Managing Director and General Manager of the Sanwa Bank, Ltd. (New York Branch). After graduating from Hitotsubashi University, he joined the Bank in 1961. His earlier foreign assignments include being the Chief Executive of Sanwa International Limited in London and President and Chief Executive Office of the Sanwa Bank, California. In Tokyo, he was the General Manager of the International Department. He is a member of the Board of the California Chamber of Commerce.

RICHARD ZECKHAUSER is the Frank P. Ramsey Professor of Political Economy at the John F. Kennedy School of Government, Harvard University. He is a Fellow of the Association of Public Policy Management, the Econometrics Society, and the American Academy of Arts and Sciences. His ongoing research projects are on the challenges of creating appropriate commitments, making effective decisions under uncertainty, and governing the modern corporation. He is the author of more than 120 articles and two books, and the editor of eight books. His latest book is *Strategy and Choice* (1991).

INDEX